Bluffer's®

GUIDE TO
CATS

VICKY HALLS

© Haynes Publishing 2018
Published June 2018

A CIP Catalogue record for this book
is available from the British Library.

ISBN: 978 1 78521 247 5

Library of Congress control no. 2018932894

Published by Haynes Publishing,
Sparkford, Yeovil, Somerset BA22 7JJ
Tel: 01963 440635
Int. tel: +44 1963 440635
Website: www.haynes.com

Printed in Malaysia.

Bluffer's Guide®, Bluffer's® and Bluff Your Way®
are registered trademarks.

Series Editor: David Allsop.
Front cover illustration by Alan Capel.

CONTENTS

'There is, incidentally, no way of talking about cats that enables one to come off as a sane person.'

Dan Greenberg, writer and humorist

IT'S A CAT'S LIFE

There is one thing you need to know from the beginning. The cat is the most popular pet in the world. There are hundreds of millions of owned cats, not to mention those that choose to live independently, and numbers are continuing to rise as emerging economies discover the delights of the feline companion. Cats have, with a little help from man, adapted to live comfortably in every continent apart from Antarctica, although it is possible that as you read this, they may well be navigating the Southern Ocean, aiming in its general direction. The cat has world domination as its ultimate goal.

Whether you like it or not, cats are here to stay and statistically you are very likely at some stage to want or need to impress a cat lover (or ailurophile, as they are also known, if you want to start establishing your bluffing credentials early on). If you need any more incentive to read on, partners are often chosen based on their response to a beloved cat, and vice versa. It pays to know how to endear yourself to the human object-of-your-affection's pampered puss.

The cat is a very enigmatic creature, which means that over thousands of years of domestication, they have given nothing away about what they are really about. If you ever approach a cat and look deep into its eyes, you can almost hear it saying, 'Yeah? Go on, clever dick, what am I thinking right now?' In fact, this book's first lesson is NEVER to stare deep into their eyes. This is highly challenging behaviour and you may not get away with it.

To paraphrase Winston Churchill, the 'riddle wrapped in a mystery inside an enigma' that is called a 'cat' is basically laughing at you. Humankind has consistently, and very efficiently, managed to learn very little about the cat as a species, maintaining a persistent state of unconscious incompetence. To quote the now-infamous words of Donald Rumsfeld, 'There are things we don't know we don't know.' What has happened in reality is that cat lovers have made it up as they go along, believing all sorts of myths and fancies about the cat's likes and dislikes, and resisting with great vigour any scientific or well-informed information to the contrary. What they think they know about cats is much more fun…for most.

Your dilemma therefore is: do you bluff the real stuff and stand up and be counted among the few who actually have an inkling of what's going on, or do you bluff the myths? *The Bluffer's Guide to Cats* will steer you through a winding path of nods to the nonsensical (why spoil a happy delusion?) via a few interesting highways of real facts. You may then choose which road to take.

The true bluffer acknowledges the enigmatic nature

of the cat and is equally enigmatic regarding his or her own knowledge on the subject. True to the bluffer's credo, this is very much a question of not so much what is said but what is left out. If you nod slowly, with a suitably thoughtful expression, for a sufficient period, you may stop a conversation in its tracks before it really gets started. If you feel something still needs to be said, you can use one of the 'feline fillers' listed at the end of each chapter to act as a subject changer. If all else fails, you can always go with the ultimate showstopper: 'But of course, can we ever say the cat is actually domesticated…?'

'I have noticed that what cats most appreciate in a human being is not the ability to produce food… but his or her entertainment value.'

Geoffrey Household, British thriller writer

Science moves on and facts cease to be facts, replaced by new facts that also have an inevitable shelf life (*see* Samuel Arbesman's *The Half-Life of Facts: Why Everything We Know Has an Expiration Date*). This guide will inform aspiring bluffers based on the current 'facts' and popular beliefs, always ensuring that you avoid serious full-on debates. Far better to maintain a dignified silence, interspersed with one or two fairly indisputable observations, to ensure the audience is kept guessing about the true expert in the room. Whatever you do, always speak with confidence and authority – the true key to successful bluffing.

With those basic thoughts in mind, enjoy your journey of discovery.

YOUR FIRST 'FELINE FILLERS'

Famous ailurophiles (cat lovers)

Sir Winston Churchill, Abraham Lincoln, Charles Dickens, Nostradamus, the Duke of Wellington, Queen Victoria, Sir Isaac Newton, Florence Nightingale, Beatrix Potter, Monet, William Wordsworth, Horatio Nelson and Victor Hugo.

Quote whichever name you feel best suits the audience, for example Horatio Nelson if you are at the Yacht Club, or Nostradamus in the company of conspiracy theorists.

FELINE TIMELINE

It is always useful to show knowledge of taxonomy (classification of species), just in case you find yourself in the kind of situation when the word 'cat' is replaced with 'feline'. Many within the veterinary and cat welfare fields will use the term 'cat' or 'feline' interchangeably, but it generally goes no further than that. You may, however, wish to impress your peers when visiting natural history museums or zoos, in which case you might need to quote from the following (take a deep breath, and memorise as much as you can): all living organisms are classified into class, order, family, genus and species. The domestic cat is classified as a carnivorous (order = *Carnivora*) mammal (order = *Mammalia*) of the *Felidae* family. This includes the sub-groups (Genera) of *Felinae*, *Pantherinae* and *Acinonychinae*. The *Acinonychinae* has a sole member, the cheetah (so called because its claws do not retract) but the *Pantherinae* family includes the lion, tiger, panther, jaguar and leopard. The *Felinae* includes all the small cats, for example lynx, serval, ocelot, caracal, jaguarundi, jungle cat and Pallas's cat (a sufficient number to remember to underline your knowledge). The pet cat is a domesticated subspecies of *Felis silvestris* known as *Felis catus*. You may never need to use this fact but it sets the scene for your further journey into the modern domestic cat and its evolution.

SURVIVAL OF THE *FELIS* FITTEST

The theory of evolution suggests that the type of animals that survive are those that change and develop to take advantage of the varying climates and conditions on Earth. Few have managed this better than the cat. All carnivores evolved from the miacids, small weasel-like carnivorous forest dwellers that might just have had retractable claws, or *protractile* claws to be strictly accurate (because they extend *and* retract), just like the domestic cat we know and love today. Many of them became early versions of 'cat', the most renowned being the sabre-toothed tiger with its massive scythe-shaped upper canines. One thing is for sure, the tabby cat was not once a sabre-toothed tiger – the species became extinct over 13,000 years ago. It is generally agreed that all cats can trace their ancestry back to the Pseudaelurus, a medium-sized cat-ish animal that roamed central Asia some 11 million years ago. By 3 million years ago, a variety of felines existed that were similar to those of today but even more diverse. That exhausting yomp through time brings you to the present day.

CATANATOMY

Certain aspects of the domestic cat's anatomy and physiology have modified and adapted through the process of evolution to best suit its environment and role in nature. Whether a cat lives wild or in pampered luxury with a loving owner attached, it is still built the same and its ability and drive to behave in a particular way does not change. If you really want to get a true insight into cat behaviour (or at least what it should be doing instead of lying on its back in front of the fire), you must start with the basics by exploring how the domestic cat is constructed.

'In the beginning, God created man, but seeing him so feeble, He gave him the cat.'

Warren Eckstein, leading pet behaviourist

The domestic cat (henceforth referred to as 'cat', with no passing reference to lions, tigers, etc.) is a small, furry creature, mostly weighing between 2kg and 5kg as an adult, unless grossly overweight or a member of a larger than normal breed (*see* 'Good Breeding'). They stand about 12 inches (27cm) tall, on average, at the shoulders and have a long tail and a leg at each corner. There are, however, exceptions – some cats have three legs, no tail and/or no ears, all due to veterinary intervention to remedy accidental damage or disease. It is best, when confronted with one of these modified versions, that you show no surprise (definitely not amusement or distaste) but acknowledge to the owner the incredible adaptability of the species and enquire politely as to the cause of the loss. (Whatever you do, don't wonder out loud if it answers to the name of 'Lucky'.) Mostly you will not notice the loss of limb or tail when the cat is moving at speed, and the 'no ears' thing just makes a cat look like an angry otter. It has no impact on their ability to hear.

They also come in a variety of colours and patterns, the most common being black, ginger, tabby (stripes, usually light brown on dark brown but can also be grey or ginger), black and white, and tortoiseshell. Some fancy pedigrees have dark faces, tails and feet in contrast to the colour of their body, referred to as 'points' – more of that to come in a later chapter when you can immerse yourself in the glamorous world of the 'pure breeds'. Eyes are green, blue, amber or odd (coloured, not peculiar), and always enigmatic. Coat length can vary from long and high-maintenance to short and curly; most cats have perfectly manageable short and soft fur.

In comparison to their human companions, cats are super-sensory: they smell things we can't, like the scent of another cat on your trousers (you have been warned) or small traces of faecal matter on the front door mat where you have wiped your shoes. It is virtually impossible to eat cheese (a particular favourite for many) within a 50-metre radius of a cat without the aroma attracting its attention. Cats hear ultrasonic sounds beyond the range of our own hearing; they feel vibration through their feet and whiskers that is so faint we remain oblivious. If you are ever in San

Francisco or any other earthquake zone and a nearby cat starts to look agitated you would be right to be very afraid and would be well advised to dive under a sturdy table. It is this heightened sensory ability that leads many people to believe the myth that cats have a supernatural sixth sense. You will earn your bluffing credentials by pointing out that, in reality, cats are just so much more tuned in to their surroundings than humans are.

The cat is such a uniquely assembled creature that its features are worthy of referencing to confound and amaze those around you. Feel free to quote the following at any social function where the subject of 'cat' comes up (if only because you have brought it up). In some circles it is never further away than 'What line are you in?' or 'Where do your children go to school?'

Nose
- A cat's sense of smell is estimated to be 14 times more powerful than that of a human. If this isn't astonishing enough, you can always resort to 'Did you know that they have 200 million cells in their noses that are sensitive to odour?'

- A cat has a second organ of scent in the roof of its mouth called the vomeronasal or Jacobson's Organ, enabling them to 'taste' extremely significant smells (usually urine, but you can leave that part out if you like).

Eyes
- Cats can't see objects clearly that are less than 20cm away. Strange, but true.

- Cats have a reflective membrane (*tapetum lucidum*) at the back of their eyes which enables them to make maximum use of low light conditions, hence the 'see in the dark' belief.

Whiskers

- Whiskers are called vibrissae. Cats have 24 of them on each side of the nose, over the eyes, on the chin and, surprisingly, on the back of each foreleg.

- Whiskers aid hunting, moving forward to accurately detect the position of prey when they are close (being so long-sighted, this is pretty essential).

Teeth

- The adult cat has a total of 30 teeth: 12 incisors (the little stumpy ones at the front), 4 canines (the long 'fangs' at the top and bottom, but don't call them fangs if you want to retain any credibility), 10 premolars and 4 molars.

- Cats lose their baby teeth (call them 'milk' or 'deciduous') between five and six months of age when they are replaced with the adult set.

Tongue

- A cat's tongue is very rough, almost like sandpaper (be prepared for this if you plan to get up close and personal). It is covered with over a thousand tiny tooth-like spines called papillae.

- These hook-shaped spines are used for keeping the cat's coat groomed and for removing fur and feathers from prey.

Brain

- The cerebellum in the hindbrain, coordinating balance, posture and movement, is comparatively large in the cat. This may be a useful thing to know next time you see a cat fall from a garden fence and land on its feet.

- Cats are emotional creatures, feeling a complex range of negative and positive emotions beyond primitive fear and aggression (you can quote advances in neuroscience here as your proof). If you feel that you are likely to be asked to expand on this, you might want to use as an alternative, 'Did you know that the brain of the average cat is 5cm long and weighs 30g?' This is unlikely to stimulate further discussion.

Ears

- The cat's outer ears are called the pinnae (those parts that get removed from time to time, *see* above), each controlled by 32 separate muscles to enable 180-degree independent rotation to turn towards the direction of a sound. Amazing.

- The angle of the cat's ear is an important indicator of mood. Never ever approach a cat if its pinnae are flattened, rotated backwards or impossible to see. Admittedly this will be a shame for the warm and friendly pinnectomized* cat mentioned previously, but why take the chance?

Skeleton

- The skeleton is supported by long, lean muscles giving great flexibility (can you lick your own bottom? Or even want to?) and jumping prowess.

- The cat has no collarbone; it has instead 'free-floating' clavicles which give it the ability to spatchcock itself and get through impossibly small gaps. Useful for survival and tough on small mammals taking refuge under a loose floorboard or gap behind the cooker.

Paws

- A cat walks on its toes. Refer to this as 'digitigrade', but practise the word first in front of a mirror before uttering it in public as it's a tricky one and tends to result in involuntary dribbling.

- Cats have a small pad on their wrists called the stopper pad, used as an anti-skid device, allegedly, while jumping. (Cool quote for petrolheads.)

Tail

- The cat uses its tail as a balance (bad news for the surgically or congenitally tail-less version).

---

* If you are struggling with the word pinnectomized, break it down and you get pinn = ear and ectomized = chopped off surgically.

- The cat is the only feline species able to hold its tail vertically while walking – a very good sign if you are approached in this way as it means it's happy and has no intention of taking your face off.

As a final word on evolution: if you find yourself in the company of creationists, you may want to adapt the quotation on page 11 to 'God created cat; everything else was downhill from there.' It might well meet resistance from your audience, but where's the fun in not living dangerously from time to time?

FELINE FILLERS

Famous ailurophobes (cat haters)
Napoleon, Mussolini, Hitler and Genghis Khan.

*'Thousands of years ago,
cats were worshipped as gods.
Cats have never forgotten this.'*

Anonymous

DOMESTICATION AND DEIFICATION

PAW IN THE DOOR

There is some debate about the timing of the domestication of the cat, so you can acknowledge here that new archaeological evidence is being found every year and modern theory will change according to that evidence. Genetic research published in 2007 claimed to prove that domestic cats derive from five feline founders from the Near East (Iraq, Libya, Syria, Israel, Kuwait, south-eastern Turkey and south-western Iran) in the earliest agricultural Neolithic settlements, potentially 10,000 years ago or more. The descendants of these five founders were then transported across the world with human assistance. The use of the words 'genetic research', 'Near East' and 'Neolithic settlements' will probably enable you to hold the floor on this subject, but be wary of getting carried away – best to stick to the Egyptian stuff that most people know and love.

Most avid cat lovers will at least have read that, as traditional nomadic lifestyles ceased, the storage of crops became more essential. This grain attracted rodents and the rodents attracted wild cats. These cats, resembling today's African wildcat (*Felis silvestris lybica*), were encouraged to stay, certainly by the Egyptians, by feeding them scraps. The presence of an abundance of food, both scavenged and caught, and no predators or deterrence from humans meant that cat colonies soon formed. If you feel you have the rapt attention of your audience, you may want to expand on this by detailing your own insight into life for a cat in Ancient Egypt by including some of the following detail: all grain was stored in royal granaries and as these large concentrations of foodstuffs attracted large quantities of mice, it was essential that the pharaoh had access to as many cats as possible to protect the precious commodity. It would have been extremely difficult to confiscate everyone's domestic cats, so the pharaoh, in an obvious stroke of genius, made all cats demigods.

CATANKHAMUN

A mere human couldn't own a demigod (only a god could do that), but could look after one. At night Egyptians brought their cats to work at the granary, picking them up in the morning. For this service, they received a tax credit and were able to claim their cats as dependants, despite all cats being the property of the pharaoh. You may find that the clever dick cat lovers who have now congregated in a clowder (the collective noun for cats and always useful to know) around you are seeing the flaw in this version of history, with mutterings of 'Can you imagine taking your cat to work at the local granary and then picking him up again in the morning?' Or 'My cat would have left of his own accord before the whistle blew because he'd had enough, if he even got started in the first place.' Or 'As soon as my cat realised he was woken from a deep sleep to be taken to work with a bunch of other cats, you wouldn't see him for dust.' Or 'You'd get my cat there but never see him again as he'd move in with someone more sympathetic to the importance of his sleep/wake cycle.'

At this point, you might be well advised to laugh heartily and change the subject immediately – probably away from cats completely. If you are feeling brave, foolhardy, or even slightly inebriated, you could continue with a generalisation such as, 'Well anyway, cats were always put first in the Egyptian household. After all, people were only human; cats were demigods,' adding in a wry aside, 'Some would say that this is equally true today.'

When all the members of your audience have stopped slapping their thighs, you can back up your impressive knowledge of ancient Egyptian history by telling everyone that when a cat died, the family that housed it went into ritual mourning, shaving off their eyebrows and pounding their chests to show their outward signs of grief at the loss. The cat's body was wrapped and brought to a priest to make sure the death was natural (killing or injuring a cat was a capital crime). It was then embalmed. People came to believe that cats had a direct influence on their health and fortune. You may wish to add that many of the embalmed cats found in the tombs of the pharaohs in the early 20th century were brought back to the UK and ground up to be used as fertiliser, but if they want to see a mummified cat they need go no further than the map room in the castle on St Michael's Mount in Cornwall. Nobody really knows how it got there, so you can blithely hazard a guess. By now you may find that you have lost most of your listeners, but it's one of those cat topics that you could nonetheless hold in reserve for the right moment.

CATASTROPHE

When the human clowder has all but dispersed, you may find yourself left with one admirer who wants more information about the cat's domestication timeline, thus presenting you with an opportunity to add flesh to the bones by mentioning the journeys across the Mediterranean which enabled the cat to populate other continents. Indeed for centuries after their ancient Egyptian heyday, cats continued to be revered for their apparently supernatural powers. At this point you might deliver the phrase that you have already committed to memory, 'Cats are just so much more tuned in to their surroundings than humans are.' In fact, cats continued to be worshipped in Europe, developing an even stronger cult status and becoming involved in various religious rituals. However, there was an inevitable price to pay for having it so easy for so long. If you feel the moment warrants it, you might mention that in medieval France, cats were ritually sacrificed to ensure a successful harvest and they were also seen as the familiars of witches. The Catholic Church didn't care much for the cat either, and in the 13th century the worship of cat-like gods was forbidden. The cat was considered the manifestation of the devil and hundreds of thousands were tortured and killed, reducing the cat population by over 90%. Numbers were also affected by the Black Death, as many were culled in the mistaken belief that they were carriers of the disease. It wasn't a good time to be a cat.

But it got worse; cats continued to be ritually slaughtered or tortured well into the 19th century in various parts of Europe. Reassure what remains of your audience, though, that salvation came at last, thanks to the Victorians. In Britain, by the mid-19th century, cats were restored to their rightful position in the home, and in 1871 the first cat show took place at the Crystal Palace in south London. The organisers had clearly determined to change public perception of the domestic cat and, to a large extent, they succeeded.

CATHARSIS

You can even bring things bang up to date by commenting on the zeitgeist. For example, books about cats now have titles such as *Yoga for Cats*, *Psycho Pussy* and *Do Cats Need Shrinks?* Owners will board their cat in a hotel when they go away on holiday and keep its photograph in their purse to show anyone who is interested. Cat ownership is a multi-million pound business; a fortune is spent on veterinary bills, toys, food and even videos to entertain the bored housecat when the owner is out (the 2001 comedy *Cats and Dogs* is apparently a big favourite). Your final flourish could be, 'You can even make a diamond out of the cremated ashes of your dearly departed cat or, as the ultimate memorial, clone them using their DNA.'

If you don't wish to adopt
the role of permanent social pariah,
DO NOT say 'It's only a cat.'

Whatever you do, if you don't wish to adopt the role of permanent social pariah, DO NOT say anything before your departure that even resembles the words 'It's only a cat.' These are the words of an ailurophobe and, once uttered, can never be taken back. Be warned.

FELINE FILLERS

Superstitions from around the world
A tabby cat is considered lucky, especially if it takes up residence in your home of its own accord. This is a sign that money is coming to you.

The British believe that if a black cat crosses your path, good luck follows; Americans believe that it is bad luck.

A DAY IN THE LIFE...

Most of what a cat gets up to occurs in the privacy of its own home, but many owners are neurotic with worry about those hours when it is out of sight outdoors. Some owners may even go so far as to fit GPS tracking devices to their cat's collar, either to download information about its perambulations, or locate it if it is late home for tea. But unless a cat wears a camera, its secret life largely remains a secret. However, one can safely assume that it involves a combination of the following principal feline interests: sleeping, defecating, grooming, patrolling its territory, hunting and eating.

To understand the pet cat, it is wise to look first at the feral (a cat living wild) for insight into the natural behaviour of cats without interference or assistance from man. Feral cats hunt prey to survive. They are rodent specialists, preferring to hunt at dawn and dusk (crepuscular hunters) when their chosen targets are at their most active. They can, however, seamlessly adapt to hunting at other times depending on the prey type available or should an opportunity arise.

Depending on the availability of prey, ferals will hunt for up to 12 hours and can travel over a mile, there and back, during a single hunting excursion (which, considering how much time they remain partially concealed and motionless, is a comparatively large distance covered). Life is hard for the feral, taking as long as 70 minutes to catch one mouse at times when prey is scarce. Young rabbits are seasonally popular (as are adult rabbits in harsh winters) since they weigh on average ten times more than a typical rodent but only take five times longer to catch. The feral will always choose the option that produces the maximum return for the minimum effort. Note that for extra credibility, it is always wise to use the word 'feral' without the unnecessary adjunct of 'cat'.

'Cats are a mysterious kind of folk. There is more passing in their minds than we are aware of.'
Sir Walter Scott

You will often hear the argument that cats are responsible for depleting the bird population, but it is a fact that small mammals remain their primary food source. You may find yourself involved in a debate over the impact of cats on wildlife which has been particularly heated since a study published in 1997 by the Mammal Society estimated that 275 million animals were killed in Britain every year by pet cats. This study was actually based on flawed data from 696 unusually active cats and then extrapolated to the nation's feline population of 9 million. Flawed or not, there are still many conservationists and cat haters who demonise cats in general. In reality, there is huge disagreement regarding the impact of cats on wildlife, with many sources suggesting that cats kill mainly the malnourished or sick that would have died anyway. The subject is maybe best left alone; it tends to raise a cat's hackles – which is not the bluffer's purpose.

If a cat isn't hunting, and the majority are probably not, it is managing its territory. A 'territory' consists of the area that contains everything a cat needs to survive. The cat's core area, or 'den', is sheltered and safe from danger and is the place where it can sleep undisturbed, eat, and rest between hunting forays. This would normally be somewhere within the home and, more often than not, it is the whole of it.

In addition to the core area that forms the hub of the territory, there is an area that the cat will also actively defend against invasion by others, called the home range. Beyond the boundaries of the defended home range is the entire area over which the cat will roam and hunt for food, referred to as the hunting range. All of these areas have variable sizes which are dependent on the number of cats around and their relative aggressiveness (or otherwise).

Within the whole territory, the cat will have established paths and thoroughfares that are well trodden, often at specific times – particularly if the local cat population is high. Throughout the domain, the cat will leave its own scent marks, either by scratching with its front paws, rubbing its face on objects, or squirting urine on vertical surfaces.

There are no real mysteries as to what a cat gets up to when its owner is not around or when it's outside. It simply performs a combination of basic biological functions – marking territory, fighting (although most take great steps to avoid it) and nicking other cats' food. Some focus on mice; others think twigs or worms are appropriate prey. When a cat is permanently satisfied with food at home, it still wants to hunt but is really not bothered about the nutritional value of what it 'catches'. It is actually far easier for most to visit another cat's house and steal their food instead.

PURRFECT MORNING

A typical day for a typical cat usually starts several hours before that of the owner. The idea that a restful night's sleep is a feasible luxury for a cat owner is largely unrealistic if the cat has other plans. His natural sleep/wake cycle makes him most active at dawn and dusk (don't forget to mention the glorious word 'crepuscular' when discussing a cat's habits), so any owner leaving the bedroom door ajar at night is looking for trouble.

The cat rises at 4am, scampers upstairs at breakneck speed, and announces his presence to the owner, who eventually and reluctantly rises at about 4.07am and places a bowl of food down in the vain hope that sleep can be resumed. The cat, who has not eaten for at least four hours, sniffs the food, eats a little (why not, cats are opportunistic feeders) and then watches with a serene and impassive expression as the owner returns to bed. About 15 minutes later, the cat will arrive in the bedroom again, this time diving under the bed, spinning on to his back and pulling himself along the bottom of the bedframe with his claws. His owner rises again (it's still not 4.30am), gets a feather toy on a stick out of the wardrobe and lures the animal downstairs.

Within half an hour, the cat is bored but drowsy, and his owner is fast asleep on the sofa. At 6am, the owner wakes and returns to bed. Five minutes later, the cat jumps on the bed, purrs insistently, drools, and treads on the duvet rhythmically. Bluffers should know that this curious behaviour mimics what a kitten does to its mother's teat to stimulate milk; the drooling is in anticipation of the meal. The cat then inserts a single claw into the nostril of his owner who howls pitifully and pulls the duvet overhead to avoid further bloodshed. This is a foolish move because it reveals a toe which the cat pounces on in the belief that it's a small mammal. The owner gets up again, feeds him once more and opens the back door to let him outside. The cat sits at the door, with his owner waiting, contemplating whether or not it is safe to leave the house. A further 10 minutes go by while he makes up his mind. Five minutes later he goes outside.

It is now 6.30am and he is patrolling his territory: he sniffs all the regular bushes, fences and dustbins for the tell-tale urine trickles of the marks of his enemies. He finds several, mostly deposited by Precious from No. 9, but fortunately they were left a while ago so the coast is clear. Just to make the point, he sprays urine on the acanthus, the lavender, the barbecue and the garden waste bin, then empties his bladder completely in No. 5's vegetable patch. As the time approaches 7.40am, he empties his bowels on the side alleyway of No. 3, goes in through the cat flap and eats the remains of Sooty's food, does the same again with Stripey's in No. 5, then he returns home.

It is now 8.00am and he's howling outside the back door and repeatedly scratching on it until it is magically opened. He just manages to eat the remains of his own breakfast (not easy as he's already had two others) and then washes his face, paws and bottom, in that order. He is now ready for bed so he curls up in the back bedroom, on the guest bed, in the morning sunlight, just as his owners leave for work. He then sleeps soundly and uninterrupted for 9 hours and 47 minutes. At 6.05pm he wakes, stretches and washes both sides and his bottom, shortly after which he ambles downstairs to wait by the front door, anticipating the arrival of his owner who he is very pleased to see a short time later, rubbing round her legs and running determinedly back and forth to the cupboard in the kitchen. His owner feeds him once again. Four minutes pass and the cat is now standing by the back door, staring at his owner and mewing plaintively as finally the door is opened and he goes outside. There follows 39 minutes of patrolling, spraying urine, peeing, pooing and sitting on the shed. At 7pm he returns to his place of sanctuary and sits with his owners, who are now both at home. There is a degree of attention-seeking until, two hours later, he's out again (*see* above). At 11pm his owner calls him repeatedly for 15 minutes until he returns for the night, sleeping soundly until 4am when his Groundhog Day commences all over again.

No mystery. That's a typical day in the life of a domestic cat.

FELINE FILLERS

Did you know…?

1. The cat has an average stomach capacity of 300ml (10fl oz). That's more than half a pint of milk. Although most cats would prefer a sardine.

2. Neutered cats require significantly fewer calories (up to 40% less) to maintain their body weight than their fully intact counterparts.

ß

'The smallest feline is a masterpiece.'

Leonardo da Vinci

GOOD BREEDING

There is a whole new world that you will need to know about if you want to be a champion cat bluffer, and that is the world of pedigrees and cat shows. Initially, the intention of Harrison Weir, the organiser of Britain's first cat show in 1871, was to promote the care and welfare of the cat. He had seen the neglect and abuse that they had been subjected to and, as a genuine cat lover, wanted to educate people and dissuade them from ill-treatment. Sadly he gave up judging at cat shows 21 years later because he became disillusioned about the results of his efforts, deciding that the breeders were more interested in winning prizes than promoting cat welfare. Bluffers can draw their own conclusions as to whether this situation has improved, but do not voice them out loud, either way. Cat people are notoriously touchy.

Most cats owned in the UK are referred to as 'moggies' (non-pedigree), created as-nature-intended without any human involvement. In the Victorian era, cat lovers started to selectively breed to promote particular shapes, colours and coat patterns. There were a mere handful of pedigrees in the early days, notably Persians, Siamese and Burmese. Now the official number exceeds 80. There are probably another two on the production line as you read this, with breeders constantly striving to produce the latest 'designer' variety. Modern pedigrees are undoubtedly handsome creatures (with some alarming exceptions), designed with the demands of the modern pet owner in mind. They will often gladly sit on their owner's lap, or shoulder, for hours, 'talk' back to them, walk on a lead and harness, and generally be more tolerant of life indoors in a London apartment or a suburban home. There is something in the cat world to suit every taste.

BREEDING BASICS

Anyone can become a cat breeder in theory; though it does appear to help, however, to be over 50 and fond of cat-themed sweatshirts. Pedigree kittens are registered with an organisation such as the Governing Council of the Cat Fancy (referred to as GCCF and founded in 1910), and will have to conform to certain stringent criteria relating to the particular breed. Once money is exchanged, a new owner will receive a kitten with a paper 'pedigree' that shows its parentage (known as sire and dam), maternal and paternal grandparents and so on. Closer scrutiny will often show that the kitten's father is also its great-grandfather, for example, but such is the nature of the cat breeding business. Some pedigree breeds have small 'gene pools', meaning there aren't enough of them to avoid some form of incestuous activity, but it is probably far beyond the bluffer's remit to dwell on such things.

Breeders play a fundamentally significant role in the future behaviour of their kittens; they are not just supposed to think about colour, pattern and shape. They are responsible for putting the 'pet' part into 'cat', and this they do by a process referred to as 'early socialisation'. You can astound those around you by knowing more about this process than the average breeder. Basically, cats (kittens) have a 'sensitive period' in their development when they are particularly receptive to learning about other species and new things in their environment. This takes place between the ages of two and seven weeks of age and as most pedigree cats don't leave their mothers until they are twelve or thirteen weeks old, this is solely the responsibility of the breeder.

DOMESTIC HELP

A great word to use in this context is 'habituation', a vital element of this magic socialisation process. Essentially this involves exposing the tiny kittens to as many sights, sounds, tastes, textures and smells as might be encountered in a normal domestic environment; for example, the sound and vibration of the vacuum cleaner, or the feeling and smell of a leather sofa or fabric chair (ripe for the scratching). Exposing the brand-new kitten to all it might encounter, in a responsible and gradual way, is a sign of good breeding practice. This is something you need to know for those occasions when your neighbour laments the general temperament of her new Mongolian Kittypoo (that particular breed doesn't exist yet but give it time). You can ask sympathetically,

'Do you know what the breeder's socialisation protocol was?' In this way, you can appear both knowledgeable and compassionate in the same breath.

There is nothing more insulting for a pedigree owner than to have their beloved puss mistaken for an inferior beast.

The next important phase is recognising all the mind-boggling variations that represent individual pedigrees. It is easy even for the genuine experts to get it wrong from time to time, but you can always avoid making a mistake by never being tempted to hazard a guess about a pedigree in the first place. There is nothing more insulting for a pedigree owner than to have their beloved puss mistaken for, in their opinion, an inferior beast. If in doubt, and this will inevitably be the majority of the time, do not consider bluffing about a cat's provenance until the owner proudly declares what it is.

Before committing the following details about the most common cat breeds to memory, here are a few general points:

Most pedigrees have a lifespan of between 12 and 15 years, with some a little less and some a little more. Needless to say, it's a lottery but some, particularly the Siamese, can live into their 20s (although they're not a pretty sight towards the end).

If anyone tells you that the hairless breeds (*see below*) are hypoallergenic, just state confidently that there is no such thing. It's the protein in cat saliva, skin and sebaceous glands that people are allergic to, so no amount of shaving or breeding follically challenged mutations will help. If it works for some, it is entirely possible they were not allergic in the first place.

Generally, pedigree cats cost a lot of money and some, for example the Toyger ('toy tiger'), look just like (and probably are) tabby moggies. There are fads for miniature cats, long-haired cats, big-eared cats, dwarf cats – just name the mutation and there will be a market for it. In addition, it's good to know that pedigree cats come with a long list of inheritable and congenital diseases, which is not something potential owners will see on a breeder's website. These are emotive subjects within the cat world, so avoid them. But feel free to mention the last point to those in the market for a new pedigree cat as this will enhance your 'expert' credentials.

AN A–Z OF CAT BREEDS

Here is a quick zip through the most common pedigree cat breeds with just enough information for you to sound reasonably well informed when they are mentioned.

Abyssinian Quite a pretty medium-sized, short-haired cat with a 'ticked' coat (that just means a different colour at the end of the hair shaft). The long-haired version is called a Somali, and its coat would be profoundly unsuitable in the country from which it takes its name.

Asian A Burmese (*see* below) but in a different colour – see how confusing this is? Short-haired but also available in semi-longhair, called a Tiffanie. A black Asian is called a Bombay.

Balinese Classified as a semi-longhair (think Siamese with more hair). It also has colour-points (dark bits at the ends – feet, head and tail).

Bengal This is a short-haired, strikingly spotted cat, bred originally as a hybrid between an Asian Leopard cat (wild) and a domestic cat. The Bengal has become extremely popular and generated the Toyger as an alternative 'colourway'. The early generations (father, grandfather or great-grandfather was a wild cat) are referred to as F1, F2 and F3 respectively. Feel free to suck in through your teeth and shake your head if you meet anyone who proudly announces they are the owner of any of these 'Fs', because you will be aware that a pet Bengal should be at least four generations (F4) removed from the wild cat if you want a peaceful life. If anyone you know is considering moving house with their cat to a neighbourhood with a Bengal in it, you can demonstrate your knowledge of these things by shouting 'NO!' very loudly. Bengals are known for their thuggish behaviour, and one will think nothing of breaking and entering and beating up the resident cat AND owner before leaving with an evil grin on its face. Of course, to show your impartiality, you should indicate that many Bengals are an absolute delight, and leave hanging the matter of whether or not you would take the risk of owning one....

Birman A semi-long-haired cat with blue eyes, colour-points and white feet (extra points if you refer to these as gloves, socks or gauntlets).

British Shorthair A stocky cat (always use the term 'cobby' rather than 'chunky' or 'fat') with a thick coat in a variety of colours. You will easily spot a BSH, as they always look like you've ruined their day when you walk into the room.

Burmese A well-loved short-haired cat with a loyal following. Don't be surprised if anyone says they have a chocolate, blue, red or lilac one – these are all real colour options. This is a cat with a dual personality; it will sleep like a baby in its owner's arms yet fight outdoors with the neighbour's cat like a thing possessed. The Burmese can be really noisy (those in the know prefer to say 'vocal'), but this is considered a good thing by many fans of the breed.

Burmilla This is a cross between a Burmese and a Chinchilla (the cat, not the crepuscular rodent); it could just as easily have been called a Chinese, but that would have been confusing.

Chinchilla Effectively a Persian with a white coat and black tips at the end of the hairs; used to make half a Burmilla.

Cornish Rex Bred originally from a kitten with a genetic mutation (feel free to use this term at will although genetics are dangerous territory for the bluffer) that resulted in a curly coat. These cats look like a cross between a good-looking version of Steven Spielberg's ET and a lamb from a poorly nourished ewe. They do, however, have big characters to make up for their looks.

Devon Rex As the above although slightly less good-looking.

Egyptian Mau A spotty cat with a slightly worried expression.

Exotic Shorthair A Persian without the expensive hairdo.

Japanese Bobtail A long-legged cat with a tail like a pig's with a pom-pom on the end. Definitely an acquired taste.

Korat With the Korat you are stuck if you don't like the colour grey; no choice on this one.

LaPerm Exactly as the name describes, this cat looks like it's having a bad hair day every day.

Maine Coon The Maine Coon is the largest breed of cat with semi-long hair, tufted ears, and an Elizabethan-style neck 'ruff'. It's a real man's cat as hunting, shooting and fishing is its speciality. You would earn a ripple of appreciation for your knowledge if you suggested that they would make excellent feline blood donors, as this is indeed the case. Since you are asking, yes, cats do need blood transfusions so others inevitably need to give it at some stage.

Manx Another breed born of a mutation, the Manx has slightly longer legs at the back and the remnants of a tail that, according to the size of the stump, are referred to as rumpies, stumpies, stubbies or longies (you couldn't make this up).

Norwegian Forest Cat Semi-long-haired and looks like a Maine Coon, but you should never get the two confused or refer to the resemblance while in the company of a Norwegian Forest Cat or Maine Coon breeder.

Ocicat Mix a Siamese with an American Shorthair and an Abyssinian and you get a cat with spots that looks an awful lot like an ocelot, hence the name.

Oriental Longhair A semi-long-haired breed born of a coupling between a sorrel (coat colour) Abyssinian and a seal (dark brown) point Siamese.

Oriental Shorthair This is basically a Siamese with green eyes and a coat that comes in a wide variety of colours and patterns.

Persian A cat with a luxuriant coat that is extremely difficult to maintain. These cats often love to spend time outdoors but will come in with all sorts of grubs and wildlife stuck in their coat. They are bred as an 'indoor' cat (if that isn't an oxymoron, but never of course even think about suggesting it may be). In order to be happy sitting doing nothing, they do not have a 'bright' gene. That is purely for reference and not for discussion in Persian-related company.

Ragdoll There is a common misapprehension that Ragdolls feel little pain, squeak, and go limp when picked up. This is not true. Incidentally, they look just like Birmans.

Russian Blue Easily confused with a Korat ('blue' means 'grey' in the pedigree world).

A quick scan of the internet would suggest the Scottish Fold's appeal lies primarily in its ability to look fetching in hats.

Scottish Fold Another mutation that results in the cats having pinnae (think the earless cats mentioned earlier) that are folded forward and down, rendering them prone to ear parasites and hearing difficulties, and painful degenerative joint disease. Their popularity may be a mystery to most on that basis, but a quick scan of the internet would suggest their appeal lies primarily in their ability to look fetching in hats.

Selkirk Rex Devon meets Cornwall meets LaPerm sort of cat.

Siamese The Siamese used to be a normal-shaped cat with colour-points and a slightly elongated skull shape that made it look oriental and exotic. Modern Siamese are rather more extreme with super elongated faces, skinny bodies and whippy tails. They often have neurotic natures to match, but they are one of the oldest and consistently popular breeds of all time. To compensate for the backlash against the new-style Siamese, the 'old-fashioned', which reverts back to the less angular Siamese of bygone days, was created. A terrible stigma was attached to the breed in the wake of the Disney cartoon *Lady and the Tramp,* resulting in a widespread distrust of Siamese cats.

Siberian Think Norwegian Forest Cat.

Singapura Officially the world's smallest breed of cat; looks like a tiny, round-faced Abyssinian.

Snowshoe Birman- and Ragdoll-esque.

Sphynx A hairless breed. As previously alluded to, this cat has folds in its skin, no whiskers and looks like a Rex with no hair and depression. If you search on the Internet, you will find examples of Sphynxes that have got tattoos and body piercings. Most if not all experts (and therefore bluffers) are suitably outraged, especially given that the wee beasties are actually charming little creatures.

Tonkinese Siamese crossed with a Burmese.

Turkish Angora The Turkish Angora has a silky, medium-length coat. Its eyes can be amber, blue or odd (one of each colour) for those who can't make up their minds.

Turkish Van An orange and white semi-long-haired cat that swims.

OTHER BREEDS

Probably without exception, none of the following breeds are recognised by the Cat Fancy (as the afore-mentioned GCCF is colloquially known), some for an extremely good reason. Although there is absolutely no excuse for breeding cats that are mutations or have a congenital defect that could in some way affect their quality of life, there are always 'niche markets' for something different. You can freely assume airy indifference about the following: American Bobtail (very short tail), American Curl (ears curl backwards), American Shorthair (a little like the British version), American Wirehair (like the shorthair with a wirehair coat), Chausie (a large African Jungle Cat hybrid), Cymric (long-haired Manx), Kohana (a completely hairless Sphynx), Munchkin (you might say 'a sad and immoral mutation', but tread carefully), Peterbald (hairless), Pixie-Bob (most have extra toes) and Savannah (a hybrid between an African Serval and domestic cat).

If you do find yourself at a cat show, you need to

prepare yourself for the following. Cats are kept in small cages that are dressed to a theme – for example you may see a Martian landscape next to a 19th-century boudoir scene. The cats generally are either screaming or catatonic. The breeders sit on small stools in front of the cages, usually knitting (both sexes). A couple of important-looking people walk round wearing white coats and gripping a bottle of hand cleanser. These are the 'judges'. When judging begins, the cat is taken out of its cage and held up (it looks vaguely sacrificial) with the body extended and the legs splayed out. The cat is then placed in a series of unusual postures to ensure all its various bits are in the right place and of the right colour and shape. If the judge is not bitten during this process, the cat will score highly. At the end of the judging process, the winning cats are awarded rosettes and referred to as 'Grand Champion' and similar grandiose titles, and henceforth command impressive stud fees.

There are few reasons why a bluffer would be at a cat show by accident, if at all, but if you have been persuaded to attend and wish to demonstrate your 'expertise', you may also find the following tips useful:

- If you hear an announcement for an owner to return to their cat because it is in distress, do not show alarm. This is normal at a cat show.

- Never discuss inheritable diseases or the psychological drawbacks of keeping cats exclusively indoors, or you may well be verbally or physically attacked.

- Do not make eye contact with the cats (or with the breeders).

- Do not laugh at the themed cages; the cat will take it personally, as if being in there isn't suffering enough.

- Yes, cat lovers do pay £1,000 for an indoor cat climbing frame. You need to get over that to mix in the world of cat.

- No, dressing up your cat is never acceptable unless it is for medical reasons.

- If you see anyone pushing a tartan shopping trolley, DO NOT make any enquiries regarding the contents.

- Do not stare at the stains on the breeders' sweatshirts – try to think about Nutella and camomile tea spillages rather than dwelling on your genuine suspicions.

- You have now survived your first virtual cat show. You may or may not wish to repeat it for real, but don't worry if your natural instinct is to decline. You are in good company.

FELINE FILLERS

Famous contemporary ailurophiles

Halle Berry, James May, Ozzy Osbourne, Ricky Gervais, Rick Wakeman and Jonathan Ross.

CHARACTER REFERENCE

So, what is a cat really doing when it's exhibiting 'typical' cat behaviour, and what does it truly think of its human hosts? Most cat owners have no particular interest in delving in great depth into feline psychology because they have a relationship with their own cat and they flatter themselves that they know EXACTLY what it is thinking all the time. They're wrong, and so will you be unless you do some homework.

No matter what humans do to them or with them, cats still share certain common characteristics. First and foremost, they are carnivores and they hunt, catch, kill and consume prey. There is no such thing as a vegetarian cat. You can go further, should the topic arise, and say they are 'obligate' carnivores, meaning they require protein from an animal source to survive – always an interesting topic with vegetarian or vegan cat lovers. Effective hunters need excellent vision and hearing, patience, sprinting and jumping prowess and, most importantly, lethal weaponry. As you already know (if you are reading this book sequentially), the cat has claws that protract, meaning they extend from the sheath when required, so most owners remain relatively unscathed, though some have been known to fall foul of the claws and teeth when their cats are 'in the zone'. It should be common sense that an animal that is motivated and driven by the sight, sound and movement of prey, especially at dawn and dusk, makes a dangerous bedfellow. Another consequence of this, of course, is that when the lovable pet goes outdoors, it is very likely to come back with anything that might once have had a pulse. When visiting a cat lover's house, do not be alarmed to see a succession of the corpses of many different creatures, including mice, voles, shrews, rabbits, rats, squirrels, frogs, slow worms, lizards and birds. You will undoubtedly assume heroic status if you know the drill to follow when something is brought in that still has its pulse. Cats that are well fed still hunt, but some lack the inclination to kill and consume and are content with roughing them up a little in the comforts of their home.

MEALS THAT MOVE

1. Remove the cat from the scene.

2. Put gloves on! Either garden gloves or, if they are not available at short notice, oven gloves will do nicely, as this drama often unfolds in the kitchen.

3. Prepare a suitable receptacle for transportation, e.g., box or jar with lid, etc. Try to avoid saucepans – you

might be distracted, and forget that you have guests staying.

4. Locate and isolate the victim. If possible, move it into a corner.

5. DO NOT follow step 4 if the victim is a rat, although there is no self-respecting rat that would allow itself to be 'brought home', and no sensible cat that would even try. Rats attack when cornered. You have been warned.

6. Cradle the victim gently from both sides and scoop. Place in receptacle, close lid.

7. Place in hidden area in garden. Open lid.

8. Keep the cat indoors for as long as possible to give the victim a sporting chance.

9. Prepare to repeat steps 1–8 when the cat brings the same victim in half an hour later.

Cats aren't just hunters – they are also solitary hunters, which means that they rarely share what they catch, and don't need the help of a pack (clowder) to bring down a proverbial wildebeest. Sharing is not big on a cat's list of priorities and that can be an enormous issue for those cat lovers who have multiple cats.

Rudyard Kipling referred to the cat that 'walked by himself', and one thing is for sure – cats are also solitary survivalists. When the chips are down, every cat is for itself. This innate self-reliance is probably where the cat's poker face comes from. Veterinary surgeons will tell you that cats are notoriously difficult to read when it comes to signs of pain, and the same can be said for stress and anxiety. This makes perfect sense, as to appear weak and vulnerable would not be a good survival strategy. This is in stark contrast to the dog, who wants the world to know about its pain.

'One is never sure, watching two cats washing each other, whether it's affection, the taste or a trial run for the jugular.'

Helen Thomson

The cat is also a territorial species, as previously mentioned. This is an issue for many cat owners for various reasons. Firstly, cats fight with their neighbours' cats, are often more attached to their 'territory' than their owner (ask any cat owner about the joys of moving house), 'mark' their territory, and may struggle if their whole world consists of a one-bedroom flat.

The super-sensory nature of the cat also comes with potential drawbacks. The simple act of an owner changing her perfume can cause some to go into meltdown. Familiarity and routine are everything for the solitary survivalist, as they represent safety: if the cat did something yesterday and didn't die, it naturally assumes that it probably won't die today if it does the same thing again. However, this could all change with the arrival of a new sofa, a new hall mat or a visit from a maiden aunt.

To make sense of the ensuing psychodrama, you could say that all cats are paranoid pessimists. Whatever their inscrutable expressions suggest, they are undoubtedly plotting and scheming – looking for subtexts, hidden gestures and conspiracies. When your new sofa is delivered, you might think, 'What an attractive fabric.' The cat, however, thinks, 'Today that sofa might attempt to kill me.' There is a subtle difference, although the cat would be unlikely to agree that there is anything subtle about the arrival of a new source of danger in its habitat.

Nowhere is there more room for misinterpretation than when cats are observed in the presence of other cats. If cats are sitting in the same room at the same time, this might be considered a good sign. You will know differently. Similarly, if a cat is sitting casually on the staircase when another cat in the household is upstairs, there might not be a perceived problem. Again, you will know differently. Cats are strategists and won't start a fight unless they have a sporting chance of winning, so standoffs and psychological warfare are rife. You can handle this sensitively by suggesting that all may not be as it appears, quoting any of the 'ethological'* content above. Cat owners will be completely unable to come back at you with a counterargument.

*Ethology, meaning 'the scientific and objective study of animal behaviour', is a very good word for bluffers to know.

But only a highly qualified professional should ever strip a cat owner of their belief system and must do so with compassion and emotional support. Be careful before entering the same behavioural minefield with your new-found knowledge, instead restricting yourself to an understanding nod that suggests, 'Cats, eh?'

CAT STEREOTYPES

The following is probably the easiest way to classify the more recognisable types of cats. It will also suggest to any cat aficionado in the vicinity that you have given the matter some thought, and thus have a convincing claim to hold yourself out as somebody who knows their feline onions. The particular idiosyncracies described are not common to all cats which might be thought to fall under one of the stereotype headings. It is important to stress that every cat is a distinct individual. This will be music to every besotted owner's ears.

Larry the Lodger

This cat does its own thing, coming and going as it pleases, but is just as likely to be indoors and fast asleep at night as out. Larry is the cat wanted by everyone who has ever said 'Cats are less of a tie than dogs.' He affects to love his owner best when he or she is opening a sachet of 'gourmet' something-or-other or making tuna sandwiches. This cat may sleep on its owner's lap in the evening (much to their delight) if the person in question is warm enough and promises to remain still. Larry is particularly smart as he pays absolutely no rent.

Ignatius the Inscrutable

Whatever Ignatius feels about life, you will never know, but you can be absolutely sure his owner is even more clueless. He has an expression that never changes; he always appears impassive (possibly, it's so hard to tell) but there are plenty of anarchic thoughts going on in his head – watch for subtle changes in behaviour, a change in the angle of the whisker by one degree or an ever-so-slight rotation of the right ear, for example. He is friendly enough – on his own terms – but rest assured that in the blink of an eye he will disappear to patrol his territory or engage in some other activity more exciting than being with you.

Barry the Beanbag

Barry gives the appearance of a bag stuffed with beans, usually rather more beans than that particular bag should comfortably hold. He sleeps on his back with his legs in the air and any substantial incendiary device going off nearby will fail to register. Barry tolerates any new cats in the home by rolling on to his side with a huff of resignation, not really mixing with them unless absolutely necessary (e.g., mealtimes). Note that sometimes, like a tortoise, he has to be helped to roll over.

Twitchy Trevor

Trevor is the opposite of Barry; he starts at the merest sound or movement, but appears confusingly relaxed at other times. He sleeps a lot indoors and tends to go out mainly when the owner is gardening or chatting with the neighbours, at which point he will show great bravado in the face of the bolshy cat from No. 3, usually from a position of safety behind his owner's legs.

Comical Clive

Who said cats don't have a sense of humour? Living with Clive provides an endless source of amusement thanks to his apparent tendency to sleep in absurd postures, get his head stuck in impossible places and fall into the toilet bowl with monotonous regularity. Clive is very much the star of YouTube. He will play with anything, and seems to have boundless energy as he skids across the kitchen floor in pursuit of something ghastly he's just found under the fridge. Owners often describe the Clives of this world as 'not quite playing with a full deck', but also tend to believe that they're merely enjoying life. The reality is that Clive is mortified about being laughed at and is plotting revenge at this very moment.

Dr Jekyll and Mr Hyde

Dr Jekyll is the most loving and affectionate cat towards his owner, yet his alter ego, Mr Hyde, is a vicious thug who appears to take sadistic pleasure in fighting, torturing and terrorising other cats. Picking on the elderly (cats or humans) is particularly entertaining. He will break into other people's homes to steal food and intimidate the resident cats. Mr Hyde is best not disturbed by the protective owners of his victims because he doesn't discriminate between cats and humans when he is on a mission of destruction and mayhem. This particular character often comes in the guise of a Burmese or Bengal.

Fickle Fanny

Fanny demands to be noticed on occasions but is distant most of the time. She is happy to have attention but it must be on her own terms – something you will hear oft lamented by owners who have had gestures of affection frequently rebuffed. Sometimes Fanny ignores you, and then for no discernible reason she can't get enough of you. This is all very confusing for those owners who like to know where they stand in a relationship, but you of course will be wise to this apparent ambivalence. The truth of it is that Fanny, like most cats, sees her owner as a useful idiot rather than a serious relational equal.

Scott the Schizo

Beware! Your lack of knowledge may be exposed if you get fooled by Scott. He rubs round your legs and then redesigns your features if you dare to touch him. Scott is the master of the mixed message; he may sit on your lap and then bite and scratch you if you dare to stroke him for a second too long. Owners believe that poor Scott must have been ill-treated as a kitten, but this is rarely the case. He is merely objecting to the fact that humans are such rubbish at speaking cat.

Shrinking Violet

Violet might as well be a lost slipper for all the time she spends under the bed. She tends to come out at night or when her owner is in the garden. If you visit, you will not see her, as she will do a record-breaking sprint when the doorbell rings, never to be seen again.

Cuddly Cuthbert

Cuthbert is definitely a neutered male (testosterone is the only thing that once made him self-reliant). He must have Velcro on his undercarriage because he spends most of his time stuck to the front of his owner's sweater. He follows her everywhere, sleeps in her bed with her, and dribbles, purrs and treads on her stomach constantly. Definitely a mummy's boy, he is prone to losing his appetite when she's away (but then of course she rarely goes away). Cuthbert would undoubtedly pine to death in a cattery, or so he would have his owner believe.

Snotty Sophie

Sophie looks like she cannot believe your audacity when you dare to touch her – British Shorthairs have got this look down to a fine art. The whole experience appears to make her feel physically sick. Sophie disappears to a private place repeatedly because she's trying to get away from humans in general.

Slasher Stan

Stanley is really rather cute and sweet until you try to give him a pill or an injection – this is definitely not a cat on which you would attempt to demonstrate your expertise in these matters. Stanley will, if restrained, develop four times as many legs, teeth and claws as normal and do his skilful best to ensure maximum shredding of any human flesh in the vicinity. Whatever anyone is trying to do to him will never be achieved unless he is anaesthetised or dead. Stanley has 'EXTRA CARE' written all over his medical records at the vet's.

Reggie the Ringmaster

Reggie will get the soft-hearted owner jumping through hoops just because he can. This is the cat that demands total compliance and has an armoury of devious ways to ensure the owner obeys at all times. The owner loves him dearly; blissfully unaware that he is definitely laughing at her when she's not looking. Your best defence in the presence of Reggie is to feign complete indifference; it is something so far outside his understanding, he simply won't be able to calibrate.

Old Obidiah

This is where cat lovers go all misty-eyed and fanciful. They believe that every now and then their lives are touched by Old Obidiah. These are cats that seem to their owners to possess a wisdom and aura more likely to be found in a Tibetan monk than a five-year-old furball. Obidiah tends to be a legendary creature that turns up on the doorstep and adjusts completely and effortlessly into the lives of the gullible. No one knows where he came from, but he will always be remembered long after he is gone. Obidiah will go for walks with his owners, meet the children from the school gates or raise spirits when his owner is down. You will hear countless tales of reincarnation of cats previously loved and lost or even the spiritual manifestation of long-dead relatives. Prepare an appropriately compassionate and knowing expression in the mirror in silent acceptance of the fact that Obidiah has definitely been here before.

Although all cats share many characteristics, in reality every cat is unique. Do not burst the bubble of any cat lover by attempting to explain their cat's behaviour in biological terms, as this will fall on deaf ears and all your hard-earned bluffing credentials will be worthless.

FELINE FILLERS

Did you know…?
You can calculate a cat's age in human terms by deducting two years from its age, multiplying the result by four and then adding 24. In other words, for those mathematically inclined:

Equivalent human age = $(\chi - 2) \times 4 + 24$ [χ = age of cat].

FELINE BAD

WHY CATS NEED SHRINKS

It is a truth universally acknowledged that, in the 21st century, pet cats do indeed require the services of shrinks. These experts come in the guise of 'Pet Behaviour Counsellors', 'Veterinary Behaviourists' or even 'Certified Clinical Animal Behaviourists', all highly qualified to provide a service to the veterinary profession so that cats that have got a screw loose or have lost the plot can be put back on the straight and narrow. The emerging profession is a bit of a minefield, as it remains unregulated and falls foul of well-meaning individuals who set themselves up in this capacity with nothing more than a lifetime spent with their own cats and a copy of any one of a number of guides to understanding cats. The one you are reading will do the job better than most.

Ironically, although by now you've gathered that the cat is a bit of an enigma, most of the behaviour that is 'treated' is actually perfectly normal. The rest of it usually results from something the owner has inadvertently taught the cat to do or because the hapless creature has emotionally combusted due to the erratic and unpredictable relational demands of a neurotic human being. Every now and then, however, the cat is actually well and truly as mad as a bat.

You will need to know a few things about employing the services of a cat shrink:

1. Any owner should seek advice from the vet first – many odd behaviours have their origins in physical rather than mental illness.

2. All good behaviourists will only work on referral from a vet and tend to have a better cat pedigree than the average Persian.

3. The internet can be a source of incredibly poor advice about what to do if your cat behaves badly. Be the voice of caution.

4. The longer an owner leaves a problem (they all hope it's going to go away), the more difficult it will be to resolve.

You can save cat lovers hours of tedious trawling of the internet by giving just one example of the quality of guidance and advice available regarding the management of 'pica' (*see* later in chapter): 'Scatter frozen day-old chicks on the carpet if your cat eats your sweaters.'

The following pages contain the briefest of summaries

of the most common behavioural problems that concern owners sufficiently to seek help, and which bluffers therefore need to know about.

AGGRESSION TOWARDS HUMANS

This has numerous causes and motivations, but the danger is that an owner can end up in hospital after being on the receiving end of a cat's bacteria-laden teeth (or even dirty claws). From the cat's perspective, it isn't necessarily guilty of malevolence. Aggressive behaviour can often result from fear, playing (albeit a little roughly), or redirecting an attack that was really intended for an external agent (such as the cat outside the window).

You can safely (and sagely) advise the owner on this basis:

Don't:
- **Scream and thrash your arms about**. Easier said than done as it hurts like hell, although it will hurt even more if the cat thinks you're fighting back.

- **Punish by smacking.** Pointless, as this will merely be seen as a counter-attack and the cat will frequently come out ahead.

- **Give as good as you get in an effort to 'show who's boss' by attempting to connect human foot with cat bottom.** Same outcome as above and everyone knows who the boss is in the relationship anyway.

- **Attempt to re-home before seeking expert advice.** There might be a simple explanation for the aggressive behaviour, and getting help might enable you to avoid passing the problem on to an unsuspecting new owner.

Do:
- **Visit the vet to rule out a medical or pain-related cause.** This will always be the first step in any strategy for dealing with aggressive behaviour, and it will show that you know your stuff.

- **Ignore the cat and do not approach it.** Threatening behaviour is frequently neutralised if ignored.

- **Wear protective clothing.** Depending on the degree of fear that an owner experiences in the presence of their aggressive cat, you can recommend anything from stout footwear to gauntlets, goggles and helmet. If you feel really creative, and a little mischievous, you can always advocate the strapping of rubber-backed bath mats around the legs as an effective anti-cat-attack device. Or you can go one step further and suggest that they invest in a hockey goalkeeper's padded suit, complete with Hannibal Lecter mask. However, it's not a good look.

- **Keep the cat out of the bedroom at night.** This might be stating the obvious for most, but you would be surprised how many people, despite being periodically lacerated, feel guilty about denying their pugilistic cat the right to sleep on the master bed.

ANXIETY

Anxiety, you will point out gravely, is a very common emotional state for many owners and cats alike. Some cats are scared of people, dogs, noises and life in general (often with good reason). This can be very frustrating for owners who simply want an uncomplicated cat that can give and receive affection. Anxiety makes that all a little unlikely.

Don't:

- **Think love will be enough.** Say this with compassion as you gently confirm that love does not always conquer all.

- **'Flood the phobia'.** This is a term for a technique employed in human behavioural therapy, the underlying theory being that a phobia is a learned fear and needs to be 'unlearned' by exposure to the thing that you fear. It is also sometimes known as 'exposure' therapy. The problem with using this technique with cats is that they are cats. You can't reason with them or rationalise their fears so to attempt such a thing would be largely pointless.

- **Pussy-foot around the house.** Ironically, this is the worst thing an owner can do as it makes them look cunning and therefore dangerous. Wholly counter-productive.

- **Reassure the cat.** If an owner reassures the cat every time it jumps at the doorbell or a car outside or a dropped saucepan lid, it will think it was right to be scared. This is not really the message you want to get across.

Do:

- **Always ignore scaredy-cat behaviour.** This is seen as odd advice by some, but focusing on an anxious cat often makes it more anxious. Anxious cats love a 'cloak of invisibility', the sense that they are actually not being seen at all rather than 'ignored'. This works on so many levels so, if in doubt, suggest 'the cloak'. Real experts will know what you're on about.

- **Behave normally.** If a cat is ever going to get used to the habitual chaos of family life, it has to see it as it really is.

- **Use synthetic pheromones.** It really sets you up there with the 'experts' when you start discussing pheromone therapy. There is a synthetic version of natural cat pheromones that are secreted from glands around its face and head. They signal familiarity and security to the cat and therefore have a calming effect. For the product to work properly, however, it is often necessary for it to be part of a wider range of treatment, and you will get some admiring glances if you add a caveat to that effect.

- **Increase stimulation.** In this context it means 'play', so ensure you get that distinction across. Anything small that is fur or feather and moves will do nicely if wiggled in front of the cat. Please ensure that the object is not alive or dead. Use a cat toy, or a ball of wool.

EXCESSIVE SCRATCHING

Scratching in this context isn't something done to relieve an itch, but what cats do to keep their claws in razor-sharp condition. A cat will lean against a vertical surface like a tree or, if the owner is very lucky, a scratching post designed for the purpose, and scratch downwards, removing the worn outer husk of its claws revealing sharper, new ones underneath. You will establish your expertise if you note that it is also a form of territorial marking (leaving a scent secreted by glands on the paws) and that it exercises the muscles of the forelimbs. Sadly, it also ruins antique chaise longues, carpets and other expensive household furniture. You could save your cat-owning friends a fortune by recommending the following:

Don't:
- **Throw things or shout.** The cat will then start scratching even more destructively in secret just to prove a point.

- **Use aerosol repellents designed for the purpose.** These smell absolutely disgusting and will only be effective if they are used repeatedly, at which point the whole family will be looking for alternative accommodation.

- **Buy a short scratching post.** Many pet stores sell short scratching posts because they take up less shelf space, but they are largely useless unless the cat is about six inches tall.

Do:

- **Provide the right number and type of scratching posts.** The right number would be at least as many as there are cats in the household. The right type would be as tall as possible, covered in sisal rope and absolutely rigid, as there is nothing worse than a scratching surface that doesn't resist when a cat pulls against it.

- **Use effective deterrents.** You can safely recommend low-tack double-sided adhesive tape stuck over the scratch-damaged area, making sure you emphasise that the tape be 'tacky' rather than something that the cat will adhere to permanently. You can also recommend the use of Perspex sheeting, which is the least exciting surface to scratch, if not exactly high in aesthetic appeal.

HOUSE SOILING (INAPPROPRIATE URINATION AND/OR DEFECATION)

This is a big one. You may not be aware of it, but the nation, behind closed doors, is awash with cat urine. A cat's stress seems to travel direct to its bladder or bowel with disastrous consequences. You could be a saviour with a few well-chosen nuggets of advice.

Don't:
- **Rub its nose in it.** An old wives' tale; utterly pointless.

- **Smack the cat.** To emphasise again, this only makes the problem worse.

- **Bleach the soiled areas.** In pursuit of destroying 99% of all known germs, this is a common technique, but usually only encourages the cat to return to a spot which smells even more like a toilet.

- **Use malodorous or other deterrents.** Scattering orange peel, tin foil, newspaper, plastic sheets, pine cones and pepper, as recommended on the internet is pointless and just exacerbates the problem as the cat finds somewhere else to urinate instead.

- **Put soil in a litter tray.** Messy, and it doesn't work.

- **Do nothing**. An option chosen by many as they silently enter denial. Try to encourage them to seek help.

Do:
- **Visit the vet.** This lesson is well learnt. House soiling cats can be sick cats.

- **Provide an indoor litter tray.** Always a good solution for those cats who are too scared to pee outdoors because of a new cat in the area. Just don't fill it with garden soil.

- **Get extra litter trays.** The gold-standard recommendation is: 'One tray per cat plus one extra per cat positioned in different locations.' It's all about tactics that cats employ when they don't get on...but you don't need to know more than this. Just give the impression that you know that house soiling is often tactical.

- **Get a second litter tray for single cats.** Some refuse to visit the same cat lav twice.

- **Change the litter substrate** (always say 'substrate' – much more impressive than saying 'litter') to a fine, sand-like material. You then remind anyone who's interested that all cats share a common ancestor with the African Wild Cat.

- **Remove litter liners and litter deodorants.** Cats can be fussy and plastic that gets stuck in the claws and the lingering essence of Alpine Meadow are not conducive to a good bowel motion.

- **Clean the soiled areas.** There are products created specifically to remove all trace of cat urine – it's big business.

- **Ask the vet for a referral to a cat behaviour counsellor.** A good cat shrink should be on speed dial.

INTER-CAT AGGRESSION

In an ideal world, all cats would love each other and never fight with their neighbours or siblings. This is of course never going to happen. How many times have you heard: 'Fluff and Fang just don't get on. Never have, and never will.'

'The mathematical probability of a common cat doing exactly as it pleases is the one scientific absolute in the world.'

Lynn M. Osband, cat expert

With over 9 million domestic cats in the UK, high population densities and an increase in multi-cat households, disharmony reigns in many homes and neighbourhoods. Cats in the same house either fight, avoid each other, spray urine in the toaster or are guilty of other anti-social behaviour. This is hard to live with and those people who are victims need your help and advice.

Don't:
- **Get uptight.** Stressed owners increase the tension in the home and therefore the risk of conflict between the cats.

- **Use arms or legs to break up a fight.** It seems

obvious, but people try this and get hurt. Feel free to save the day with a blanket, broom or large cushion. Regarding the broom, this is not for clubbing the aggressor over the head; just push it slowly but firmly between them.

- **Divide the house and separate the fighting cats forever.** It is a strategy for the terminally desperate, and family members frequently end up showing allegiance to their favourite cat and living apart in the same house. Strange but true. Cats can have this effect on people.

- **Put them both in cages and place them side by side to get used to each other.** How would you feel if you were incarcerated in a cage next to the individual you hate most in the world?

- **Shut them in a room and let them get on with it.** Tempting, but ill-advised.

Do:
- **Keep calm.** This is going to test your reserves of patience.

- **Provide sufficient 'resources' to prevent competition.** Remembering the litter tray provision, you can apply this to other important cat stuff, known as 'resources', such as food and water bowls, beds, scratching posts, hiding places and high places to which frightened cats can retreat.

- **Don't get involved.** It's a cat thing; let them sort it out, unless things take a turn for the worse, in which case get out the broom – *see* above).

OVER-GROOMING

Cats groom with their tongue but they sometimes overdo it and become obsessive, removing their fur, skin or even tail by over-zealous non-stop washing and chewing.

Don't:
- **Automatically presume it's 'stress'.** It could be but it's more likely to be medical – once again you can enforce the 'see your vet' rule.

- **Punish the cat.** Isn't it suffering enough?

- **Knit him something fetching** (on the basis that a jumper may stop the cat getting to its skin). No, don't even think about recommending this course of action.

Do:
- **Ensure effective flea control.** Fleas are miserable little parasites that infest the cat and make it itch, however regular its washing regime is. A good bluffer will recommend a trip to the vet and not the pet food aisle in the supermarket for the necessary products.

PICA

Pica is an eating disorder that means consuming something with no nutritional value that isn't and never has been food. It affects humans as well as cats. Favoured delicacies for the susceptible cat include wool, rubber, plastic, leather and cardboard. This is a bit of an Oriental breed thing and is a form of compulsive behaviour that drives a bored cat to chew and swallow expensive pieces of clothing.

Don't:
- **Punish** (you know this by now).

Do:
- **Lace the item in question with offensive flavours.** This is a long shot, but worth a try. Obnoxious substances that won't harm them include eucalyptus oil or 'bitter apple'.

- **Increase stimulation.** These cats need to hunt so whatever is needed, short of letting mice loose in the house, is worth trying.

- **Change the diet.** It's reasonable and responsible advice to suggest they might need a high-fibre diet; it makes you sound knowledgeable and it won't do them any harm. It might even work.

- **Consult a cat behaviour counsellor.** This can escalate into a life-threatening disorder that needs a genuine expert.

TERRITORIAL AGGRESSION

A word of advice regarding disputes between cats in the neighbourhood: do not get involved. Sympathise and appreciate the difficulties for the respective owners but these cases can get nasty, and far worse than 'your kid's bullying my kid' scenarios. The wise cat bluffer beats a hasty retreat.

URINE SPRAYING

Urine spraying is normal marking behaviour for a cat, but pretty unpleasant when it is directed into an electrical socket or a car's ventilation system. It should all happen outdoors, but sadly some cats get in such a pickle about safe and unsafe boundaries that it can creep indoors too.

Don't:

- **Rub its nose in it or punish.** No harm in reinforcing the message.

- **Attempt to reason with the cat.** It sounds crazy but a surprising number of people will resort to this tactic.

- **Use orange peel, tin foil or plug-in air fresheners as above.** It just creates an unpleasant odour when combined with the urine and confuses the cat even more.

Do:
- **Visit the vet to rule out urinary tract disease and get a referral to a behaviourist** (yes, there's a theme here).

There is a plethora of potential problems that owners may find concerning, however most of them can be 'fixed' – but probably not by you. They don't need to know that though. Just provide a convincing analysis, then recommend seeking expert help.

FELINE FILLERS

Cat folklore from around the world
Some people believe that cats are able to see the human aura, the energy field that surrounds each of us. So if you find one staring fixedly at you, that might be the explanation. Either that, or it's planning to spray on your foot.

If you dream of two cats fighting, it foretells illness or a quarrel.

If you kick a cat, you will develop rheumatism in that leg (not to be encouraged).

CAT WHISPERING

TUNING IN TO YOUR INNER CAT

There is nothing cat lovers like more than a 'cat whisperer'. This is a person with the almost supernatural ability to read a cat's mind. As there is so much variation in the life experiences, environments and personalities of individual cats, the chances of being irresistible to all is highly unlikely. However, this doesn't stop the enthusiastic bluffer strutting his or her stuff and giving 'cat whispering' a jolly good try.

To limit the potential for disaster, don't raise expectations ahead of your visit to a cat lover's home. If it all goes well, and you appear to build up a mutual understanding with the cat, you can make the discreet claim in retrospect. Doing your homework will also enable you to adjust your approach accordingly. For example, if your friend or acquaintance refers to his or her cat as an 'absolute tart', you will know that the creature is going to adore you and you can make all sorts of howling cat etiquette mistakes yet still be the best thing that has happened to it all day. Other similar statements include, 'He loves everyone' (no brainer), 'He's so chilled' (this cat may not be all over you, but you may be able to take liberties and keep all your fingers) and 'She's ever so sociable' (this too seems like a safe bet).

Prior to arrival, make sure you do not smell of dog or cat and that you haven't just been in a cage full of big cats or gorillas. Your odour must be as non-threatening as possible. Avoid the liberal use of aftershave or perfume, as this can be extremely offensive to the cat's sensitive nose (watch the nose wrinkle and eye squint for proof). If you want to appear particularly alluring, use the following suggestions with care. If the cat in question is a member of a 'full-on' breed such as Burmese, Siamese, or Bengal, you will want to avoid over-stimulation, as you may not be able to find the off button and could end up in a situation where you find yourself the object of persistent unwelcome attention.

BLUFFING YOUR WAY IN CAT WHISPERING

Hide a generous pinch of catnip (dried catmint plant of the variety *Nepeta cataria*) in your pocket. This usually results in the cat rubbing, rolling, licking and clambering all over you in a euphoric, loved-up sort of way. Go expensive and choose the dried variety that only uses the finest organic flowers and leaves rather than the dusty old stalks. Occasionally a cat will get hyper-aroused and have a frenzied nibble so beware of the location of your pocket to protect vulnerable parts of the anatomy nearby.

1. As an alternative to the above, place a valerian herbal 'tea' bag (the ones with hops and fennel seem to be particularly popular) in your pocket instead. Valerian is known to be an effective remedy for insomnia, so there's every possibility that the cat will nod off halfway through the love-in.

2. Put tuna juice on your pulse points (wrists, behind the ears). Be warned of course that the fishy aroma will not be so appealing to your host, especially if there is a romantic dimension to your relationship, so keep it subtle.

3. If all else fails, cheese, ham and prawns can be very popular, but secreting those about your person without smelling like a deli counter may prove difficult.

THE CAT-PERSON STANCE VERSUS THE NON-CAT-PERSON STANCE

Upon entering the home, the posture and behaviour you adopt will depend on the information you've obtained about the cat's response to strangers. If it is an automatically friendly no-matter-who-you-are sort of cat, then you will probably surprise people less if you behave like a typical cat lover. This involves crouching down on first sight of the cat and making soothing noises. At this point, you stare directly at the cat (from a safe distance) with wide eyes and extend your arm towards it with your forefinger and thumb rubbing together in rapid clockwise rotation. Simultaneously you commence kissing noises by pursing your lips together and sucking in sharply. This instruction may be lost in translation, but if you get it right you will convince your host that you are indeed a 100% bona fide cat lover. Ironically, this is the very behaviour that puts most cats off as, in their world, you will be behaving like a dangerous lunatic intent on proving to them that their paranoid pessimism is absolutely justified. Many cats tend to get used to it though and realise in a resigned sort of way that it is a human's clumsy way of saying hello.

However, a significant number of cats do not fall for this manner of approach at all, and if you have been forewarned that the cat in question is likely to be stand-offish, you would be better adopting the next strategy. This approach is very different and, to confirm your status as a natural cat whisperer, you should explain that your behaviour has a definite purpose. As you follow each step, decode your actions for maximum admiration from your host.

1. Ignore the cat completely as you arrive (in the unlikely event it didn't leave the building at the sound of the doorbell). Give the following explanation, 'Now, I know Pooky Snooky is a little shy so I am purposefully giving him the social camouflage he

craves.' This is a euphemism for, 'I am deliberately ignoring your cat but don't be offended.'

2. Walk normally, do not tiptoe or feel inclined to whisper, and give the following explanation, 'It's very important to act and speak normally because hushed tones and gentle steps can look unfamiliar and therefore potentially alarming.' This is another way of saying, 'I refuse to behave like an idiot just because there's a drama queen in the house.'

3. Sit down with your legs together, hands in your lap and eyes downcast, providing the following explanation, 'I am adopting a particularly non-threatening body language for when your cat comes into the room in order to show I am not dangerous.' If you are feeling particularly adventurous, you could try entering the living room and immediately lying on the floor, explaining that the cat will receive you better if you are at cat level. This is not an option for the faint-hearted or arthritic, or when visiting people you hardly know. You also run the risk of looking particularly stupid if Pooky has left the building and has no plans to come back any time soon.

4. Assuming that the cat is in evidence, the chances are that it will now tentatively approach you to find out what on Earth you are playing at. The old saying about cats and curiosity has more than a vestige of truth. Allow your catnip/cheese/ham/tuna juice to do the talking. Speak gently as if addressing a

newborn baby, telling the cat that it is 'beautiful' (extend the 'eau' sound as cats seem to like this). Do not touch or attempt to rush your feline friend, allowing him to make all the moves. Give the following explanation, 'I am allowing [Pooky] to explore me by maintaining my non-threatening stance.' This is another way of saying, 'I haven't got a clue what to do next, so I will allow the cat to decide what happens now while I remain perfectly still.' If the cat stalks out of the room, don't panic. Simply stroke your chin and say confidently, 'As I thought. A classic case of tactical non-engagement. Easily addressed over time.'

5. Adopt your more normal body language and way of sitting, talk normally and graciously accept the compliments flying in your direction that you are undoubtedly a 'cat whisperer' of the highest order.

If you are scared of cats, you probably shouldn't be attempting to masquerade as a cat whisperer in the first place and you will likely find step 4 particularly alarming. Fear is difficult to hide from a cat (actually any genuine emotional reaction is hard to conceal from it), so you may want to replace step 3 with more usual ebullient gestures, sprawling body language and loud laughter. You will also, of course, NOT be carrying any catnip or cheese kitty contraband; the last thing you want is to invite attraction by smelling attractive. You can then be content with explaining what you might have done but say instead: 'I know your cat is a little nervous and I'm a great believer in a cat's freedom to choose whether it socialises or not.' That will make you sound like a real champion of feline rights, which nobody can possibly argue with. One further point for the ailurophobe: you can still bluff from a distance when your palms are sweating, your mouth is dry, and your heart rate is 120. You can draw attention to the irony of your love for the cat being thwarted at every turn by the extent of your violently allergic response each time you go within 10 metres of one. Don't forget to look forlorn, sniffing a little and dabbing your eyes.

SUSSING OUT CAT BODY LANGUAGE

You can either study feline behaviour for years or take a shortcut and get the basics from the list that follows. The bluffer knows which choice to make.

Body language/posture	What the cat is thinking
Ears vertical and pointing forward, tail vertical with tip wilting to one side or quivering.	'Well helloooo! Got any catnip?'
Sitting or lying with its back to you but ears rotated towards your direction.	'I do not wish to indulge in social intercourse but I am keenly aware of you so don't try any funny business – like, for example, stroking me without permission.'
Cat crouches down on its stomach with forelegs folded under (a bit like a teapot).	'Busy doing nothing, working the whole day through, trying to find lots of things not to do, I'm busy going nowhere la la la la la…'

Body language/posture	What the cat is thinking
Cat in a teapot pose with shoulders hunched and forefeet on the ground with paws sticking outwards.	Depending on what's happening – it means either: 'Keep calm, keep calm, not entirely sure what's going on here but must look casual', or 'Good grief, I feel sick as a dog. Too much cheese I fear' (particularly if accompanied by lip-licking and a worried expression).
Cat raises up to squat on all fours with head extended, mouth open and tongue protruding. Sides start to heave and there is a rhythmical belching sound.	'Thought so....Stand back!!'
Rubbing face and body around human legs.	'Please stand still while I mark you with my scent. Do not interrupt me or attempt to fiddle with me, I'm on a mission....'
Standing on hind legs and head-butting your hand.	'Give me a stroke. Or some catnip. Or else you get sprayed.'
Leaving the room with a flick of the tail at the sound of your voice.	'Up yours! What a jerk.'
Dilated pupils (eyes look round and black).	Depending on what the rest of the body is doing, it can mean either: 'What the f...??!!' 'Oh great, a game!!!' 'I knew it. I'm going to die.' 'Someone's out to get me.'
Cat mooches in and flops on its side, looking at you.	Don't be fooled into thinking that this means, 'Tickle my tum.' Some cats learn to love this, and some don't. But why take the chance?

Body language/posture	What the cat is thinking
Cat goes on to its side with all four feet in the air, ears flattened and mouth open.	'Don't come any closer, unless you want to die.' (Get this one confused with the previous at your peril.)
Cat's tongue quickly licks its nose, followed by an exaggerated swallow.	'I have no idea what I'm doing. But neither do you. Now we both feel tense.'
Cat stares directly at you, crouched with head lowered, dilated pupils, thrashing tail from side to side.	'You who are about to die, I salute you.' Advice for you here: don't panic – just lower your gaze and very, very slowly back away.
Cat stares directly at you, crouched into a tiny space with ears lowered, tail tucked into the body and mouth open.	'Oh no. Maybe, it's my turn to die!' Advice to you here: make the cat's day and leave it alone without any need for reassurance that he is indeed safe. Just go.
Cat has dilated pupils, tail thrashing from side to side, sudden staccato movements, dashing from place to place, staring at a point on the ceiling.	Referred to as 'intermittent madness'. Don't try to analyse it. Just let it happen.
Cat has mouth gaping, upper lip curled back, nose wrinkled, remains still with a faraway expression on its face.	'Is that URINE I smell?' Called the Flehmen response (see also pages 13 and 117).
Cat stands on your stomach, treads and claws rhythmically on your chest, while purring and dribbling.	'Mum!'
Cat curled up in a typical sleeping pose, with eyes pressed shut.	'If I pretend to be asleep, they might all clear off.'

This is by no means an exhaustive list, but it gets you started. When you are interacting with any cat, you would be well advised to follow the adage 'less is more'. Keep your response brief and half-hearted (looking too keen makes you appear dangerous) and always follow the cat's lead, for example, 'You want something? Okay. You want more something? Okay...', etc.

When it comes to 'talking', there is such a wide variation in cat vocabulary that it's really difficult to learn cat without appreciating regional and even household dialects. The basics are:

Hiss = 'Back off.'

Growl = 'I said back off, matey.'

Screech = 'Are you deaf? I said BACK OFF!'

Yowl = 'I want sex.' This is common in the cat that has not been neutered. Or, in the neutered population: 'I've got all this energy and nowhere to use it up.' Or 'I've finally had it with Fang. I'm going to sort him out once and for all, right NOW!'

Miaow = Considering there are at least 19 different sounds associated with the miaow, this basically constitutes a whole dictionary of definitions, the most common being:

- 'Morning/afternoon/evening, where do you think you've been?'
- 'Feed me.'

- 'Open the door.'
- 'Danger!'
- 'Stroke me.'
- 'Brush me.'
- 'Play with me.'
- 'Entertain me.'
- 'Feed me more (oh well, worth a try).'

Chirrup = 'Hello!'

Purr = 'Loving this', or, given that many cats purr when they are in pain or even dying, 'Glad you're here, feeling a little vulnerable so I want you to know that I appreciate your support in this time of need.'

CLICKER TRAINING A CAT

There is a particular method of training animals that is becoming extremely popular. It uses positive reinforcement (always a good thing to talk about as it's the modern, good-welfare approach to training) and a unique signal (from a device called a 'clicker') that creates an important link between an action you are attempting to get the cat to perform and a reward. You could try using voice commands alone, but people talk a lot and it's not remotely clear to cats what we are saying most of the time. The sound of this clicker (a little plastic rectangular box with a metal tongue in the top) is a sharp, novel sound that is heard every time the cat does something that gets a reward.

'We cannot, without becoming cats, perfectly understand the cat mind.'

St George Mivart, 19th-century English biologist

Most people associate clicker training with dogs but, in theory, you can train any animal to perform a task or behaviour for a reward: lions, dolphins, pigs and chickens included. Cats, of course, can also be incorporated in this list if you are very, very lucky. But most of them will regard you with undisguised contempt.

The Treat
The biggest problem with a cat is getting it to do anything 'on command'. They may like tasty treats, but won't be particularly used to performing to get them. Looking cute by the fridge, they reckon, is normally enough.

If you do find a cat who simply LOVES ham, chicken, cheese or anything that is not intrinsically poisonous, you may be on to a winner. Bear in mind before you start, cats have very short attention spans. Don't bore them, and keep each 'training session' short and sweet.

The Bluffer's Guide to clicker training
To start your introductory lesson, you will need your clicker and a stick, or something like a magician's wand that you can use as a 'target'.

- Start the training session when you know the cat is hungry and have a handful of favourite treats available.

Removing food at night and training before breakfast may be a good idea but this may start the lesson with an air of resentment.

- Make a clicking sound with the clicker and, immediately afterwards, offer a treat to the cat.

- Do this a couple of times, without saying anything or touching the cat, to enable it to associate the click sound with the proffering of its favourite treat.

- Once the cat has formed an association between the click sound and the treat, you can start 'shaping' its behaviour.

- Offer the target wand to the cat. Its instinct will be to touch its nose to the end of it. Once its nose touches the wand, make a click immediately and then offer a treat.

- Try this again, only move the wand slightly further away. Once touched, click and then offer the treat.

- Allow the cat to walk away at any time. This will happen quite quickly. A five-minute session would be nothing short of a miracle.

You will, in theory, soon have a cat that responds to the wand and you can achieve a great deal by 'luring' it to desired locations to enable it to touch the wand and get its treat. The cat will soon be jumping on to, or even through, objects (forget the ring of fire) in pursuit of the target. Or, more likely, you will probably have a pocket full of soggy cheese morsels, a feeling of frustration and a cat in another room wetting itself with laughter. It's always worth a try, though....

FELINE FILLERS

Proverbs from around the world
In a cat's eyes all things belong to cats. England

Beware of people who dislike cats. Ireland

All cats are bad in May. France

UP CLOSE AND PERSONAL

At some point, being the increasingly proficient bluffer you are, you may find yourself in a situation where you will be expected to 'do things' to a cat. If those around you believe you to be an expert, they will not think twice about asking you to hold, poke, administer, bathe or handle a cat in order to perform various necessary procedures. When this happens, you have a choice: you can either do it, using the recommendations below, or you can employ an excuse that maintains your credentials but relieves you from the duty. Therefore, all the following instructions will first include valid reasons why an 'expert' would not undertake the task. If all else fails, you are on your own.

PICKING UP A CAT

There are only three reasons why you might be expected to pick up a cat in public. The first is that you are planning to buy or 'adopt' one, but as this is beyond your remit, it can be put to one side. The second is that the owner (or person responsible for the cat) has their hands full at the time and casually calls over their shoulder for you to bring the cat to them. This usually starts with, 'Do me a favour will you...?' The advice on this occasion would be, ideally, to make an excuse. Your options are:

- Pretend you haven't heard as your full attention is drawn to something else in the room or out of the window.

- Announce your intention to visit the lavatory at exactly the same time the person says 'Do me a favour'. This will give you a good excuse to leave the room and the person time to work out how to do the whole thing without your help.

- Emphasise that you are sadly allergic to cats and should avoid touching them. This may well be an excellent explanation for not having cats yourself.

- Say bluntly: 'You've got to be kidding.' (Not to be recommended if you hope to develop or continue a sustainable relationship with the owner.)

If you don't feel you can get away with any of these, your only option is to knuckle down and do the deed. Commit this step by step guide to memory:

1. Approach the cat trying really hard not to look weird. It is imperative that you REMAIN CALM and LOOK NORMAL.

2. As the cat walks away from you with brief glances behind, follow it slowly without looking menacing.

3. Once the cat has run out of places to go, attempt to position yourself behind it, i.e., approach from the rear.

4. Now you can bend and place your left hand (if you are right-handed; if not, reverse instructions) under the chest and directly behind the front legs.

5. Quickly, but without a sense of panic, place your right hand behind the back legs, just above the stifles (don't call them knees – and not to be confused with the 'hocks'). Scoop the cat upwards by lifting and as the back end drops you can support the cat with both hands; the cat remains upright and facing away from you.

6. Do not make any self-congratulatory sounds – remember that this exercise should come naturally to you.

7. Place the cat gently where required by lowering the front legs to be in line with the back so all four feet touch down roughly at the same time.

8. Remove hands and step away. DO NOT RECOIL.

Your get-out clause, given your expertise, can be used at any time during the above process if the cat looks in any way sinister, suspicious or just plain murderous. You can turn to the person who has asked you to pick it up and say: 'I don't think that's a good idea. Your cat is clearly afraid of me as a stranger and it would be cruel for me to persist.' Job done and cat expert reputation intact.

The only other reason why you might be asked to pick up a cat is if the owner (or person responsible for the cat) is scared witless of the animal and wants to use your superior knowledge to tame the beast and either remove it from the room or put it in a basket ready for a trip to the vet. With either of the scenarios, these cats are not generally likely to be in a particularly good mood so the 'I don't think that's a good idea…' get-out clause should be invoked immediately, followed by any of the aforementioned excuses.

Of course, the most useful advice in any of these scenarios is to avoid finding yourself involved in them at all costs.

GIVING A CAT A PILL

You may well have heard jokes about 'giving your cat a pill'. They involve all manner of appalling injuries to the owner and very little drug consumption for the cat. All cat owners find this familiar and frequently hilarious because it is true. If you find yourself in charge of a cat at any time and you have to give it a pill, then this is the process:

- If the tablet or capsule has to go down the cat's throat rather than be disguised in food (and generally spat out in disgust), and you find yourself with an audience for some inexplicable reason, try to do this as gently and quickly as possible to avoid bloodshed. A popular phrase in the veterinary world when it comes to restraining a cat is: 'Less is more.' You may want to chant this quietly in preparation before getting up close and personal to the cat's razor-like teeth.

- If you are on your own (shame on those around you for not mucking in), tuck the cat's body under your left arm if you are right-handed (if left-handed, reverse instructions), while trying to avoid asking yourself, 'Why am I doing this?'

- If you have come up with a reasonable answer, place the thumb and index or middle finger of your left hand (if right-handed) either side of its head at the corners of its mouth.

- Tilt the head back until the nose is pointing upwards and the lower jaw will become slack and open slightly.

- Hold the tablet between the thumb and forefinger of your right hand and use the middle finger to gently open the jaw by pulling down on the incisors (small row of teeth at the front).

- Drop the tablet to fall on the back of its tongue – accuracy is really important here. You don't get a second chance to fish the tablet out if you missed the back of the tongue.

- Close the mouth and gently lower the head, stroking the throat to encourage swallowing.

- If, at this point, the cat starts to foam at the gills like a faulty washing machine, you will know that the pill DID NOT go on the back of the tongue and is now dissolving in its mouth.

- Give up, blame the cat, and seek veterinary help.

You may also be required to administer drops and creams, to be applied to various orifices or rubbed on various bits of fur or skin. These are best avoided, unless of course you personally suffer from ear mites, conjunctivitis or a burst abscess, in which case it wouldn't be such a bad idea. You will undoubtedly end up with more on and in you than anywhere near the cat.

GROOMING A LONG-HAIRED CAT

Most domestic cats will moult (lose fur) to some extent all year round, and grooming helps them to remove the dead hair, much of which otherwise would be swallowed. This hair becomes impacted and either passes through the cat's system or is vomited up as a hairy brown sausage on the dining room carpet. This may be useful to know when an unwitting owner howls in disgust that her cat has defecated on the floor. You can politely reassure her that it is actually something that has been disgorged via the other end.

Most cats will spend a significant part of their day grooming; they can bend and flex and do the whole job efficiently without intervention. The cat's tongue, as you now know, is covered with backward-pointing spines, perfectly designed to groom coats effectively, removing loose hair and dirt.

Grooming performs several important functions, which may be helpful to discuss when you find yourself in that difficult social situation when a cat starts licking its genitals in polite company. You may mention any of the following, preceded by, 'Did you know that grooming…?'

- Removes loose hair and smoothes the coat to help insulate the body more efficiently.

- Regulates temperature in hot weather by spreading across the coat saliva that subsequently evaporates, cooling the cat down.

- Keeps the coat waterproof by stimulating glands at the base of the hairs.

- Spreads something called 'sebum' along the coat, producing Vitamin D when exposed to sunlight which is subsequently ingested by the cat.

- Spreads the cat's own scent across its body (that's why cats wash after humans touch them and mess up their own unique smell).

- Removes parasites.

Although many owners do like to groom with brushes, combs, rakes, 'mitts' (gloves with rubber bobbles) and similar devices for a mutually enjoyable experience and bonding session, most cats do a perfectly good job grooming themselves. Sadly, not all cats can be so self-reliant in their grooming habits, though, as some have been bred with coats that are virtually impossible to keep tidy without some additional assistance.

Needless to say, cats that are bred to have impossibly long and tangle-tempting coats are also those that are inherently intolerant of any grooming assistance. The Persians and similar high-maintenance breeds are most problematic – despite their squashed faces and jumbled teeth, they can still pack a mighty bite to deter your attempts. You can reaffirm your credentials as a serious bluffer by pointing out to any owner with this problem that the cat is probably very uncomfortable with all the knots, and that grooming out tangled fur can be painful, hence the aggressive retaliation. Any gesture on your part that shows empathy with the cat will always be appreciated, at least by the cat.

Rather than ever get involved in doing this yourself, you could very patiently give your best advice on how the process should be done with minimum inconvenience to all:

- Long-haired cats need to be groomed at least once a day.

- Massage the skin thoroughly before grooming by rubbing with your fingers against the hair growth from tail to head.

- Using a wide-toothed comb, groom from head to tail to remove dead hair.

- Take particular care with areas under the cat's 'armpits' (you could use the term 'axillae' or singular 'axilla' to sound extra impressive) and between its hind legs, as the skin is very thin there and extremely sensitive. It is also an area of friction where it is likely to have knots.

- Tease matts or knots apart using the fingers, working from the root towards the end of the hair.

- Avoid the use of scissors; it is extremely difficult to see where the skin ends and the hair starts when it gets really matted and blood will be drawn at some stage (not necessarily from the cat).

- Check the hair between the toes and pads for matts. Any accumulated debris can be teased out gently.

- Use a rubber mitten or pad to remove more dead hair.

- Remove dead hair on the surface of the coat with a damp cotton or rubber glove (or hand).

- Finish off with the comb again.

If grooming is a struggle, you can suggest owners try offering food treats and talking reassuringly, commencing the grooming when the cat's attention turns to the treat. For the truly lazy owner, there are a number of freestanding or wall-mounted grooming aids that encourage the cat to rub against them, thereby removing dead hair. These of course are completely useless for the high-maintenance coat, but one assumes that they can be quite pleasant for the cat.

DEMATTING

You will no doubt have seen a shaved cat before now (just look on the internet). This usually occurs because the cat in question has developed matts (thick pads of matted hair that pull on the fur so hard it removes it from the skin and the cat ends up looking like it has Fuzzy Felt wings) that can be extremely uncomfortable. Professional cat groomers or even members of the veterinary team will either manually groom or shave the matts off completely, leaving a GI-style crew cut. This sometimes requires sedation or even a general anaesthetic at the vet's (and that might be just for the owner). The end result will either be functional or deeply unattractive; in either case the cat looks stupid and generally mortified.

GIVING A CAT A BATH

Don't. If a cat is healthy, there is no reason to give it a bath. Bathing in a medical shampoo may be necessary for some skin conditions or after coat contamination with oil, tar, or other noxious substances. In which case, this is best carried out by a veterinary nurse who has the skill, equipment and patience to ensure the minimum of trauma. Any attempts on your part to dunk a cat will probably end in tears. Yours.

BRUSHING A CAT'S TEETH

Owners are routinely advised by their vets to brush their cat's teeth. This is necessary to avoid dental disease which is a major problem. Very few owners do this but plaque and tartar can build up on a cat's teeth and lead to infections, receding gums and loose teeth. Most owners will choose to have dental cleaning and extractions performed under general anaesthetic at the vet's surgery. This involves ultrasonic descaling of the teeth, the removal of any that are damaged or loose and a final polish for a pearly white snarl. It is an expensive process that could potentially be avoided if owners rolled up their sleeves and stuck a brush in their cat's mouth, using tuna flavoured toothpaste, once a day (best introduced at the kitten stage when the cat knows no better as introducing it to an adult is tantamount to self-harm).

If you have any sense of self-preservation, you will of course decline as many opportunities as possible to do 'things' to cats, in the certain knowledge that the first to see right through you will be a cat of average intelligence.

FELINE FILLERS

Proverbs from around the world

I gave an order to a cat and the cat gave it to its tail. China

Happy is the home with at least one cat. Italy

'After scolding one's cat one looks into its face and is seized by the ugly suspicion that it understood every word. And has filed it for reference.'

Charlotte Gray, novelist and historian

CAT PEOPLE

You may have noticed by now that cat people are unique creatures. They are passionate about their pets (mostly) and will either embrace an 'expert' as a kindred spirit, or resist you vehemently if you try to tell them ANYTHING about their cat or cats in general that they don't already know or believe. The chances are that you will win them over if you leave most of what you 'know' unsaid, while making it perfectly clear that you have a bank of knowledge that you have no intention of imposing on them. You will most definitely notice during your journey into the world of cat that cat lovers conform to distinct 'types'.

THE FUR-BABY HUGGER

The first type you may encounter is the fur-baby hugger, who is always a woman. She can be of any age over 30, often childless or suffering from an 'empty nest' once the kids have left home, and she has time on her hands. She may or may not be single. She may have one cat but if that cat doesn't fulfil her emotional demands, she may have acquired more in an effort to find the exact model that will permit (tolerate) her affectionate embrace. Her cat's name is usually a human one such as Emma, Lucy, Poppy, George, Sammy or Arthur, rather than Tiddles, Ginger, Sooty, Pickles, Ceefor or Splat. She may work, she may stay at home, but her prevailing thoughts are always geared towards her cat. If her cat is sick, she takes time off work. The prospect of her cat wandering off and failing to return sends her into meltdown, although George doesn't really go outside unless he is on a harness and lead. When you visit her, you will be unclear whether she is talking to you or her cat. Mostly it will be her cat, but don't be offended – it's simply because she finds the beautiful George far more interesting than you. Keep most of what you have learnt to yourself, for fear of feeding her neurosis. The fur-baby hugger always cradles her cat on its back, and invariably rocks it gently while doing so. You will notice your own interest value will increase if you show how much you appreciate George's aesthetic qualities, but don't think of approaching him, because this stereotype likes one-woman cats and George may not be appreciative of your advances. Although tempting, you will be well advised to steer clear of using terms such as 'anthropomorphism' (the ascription of human characteristics to animals) and 'theriomorphism' (the ascription of animal characteristics to humans). It'll only get confusing.

THE PERFECTIONIST

Some people are not content with being just any old cat owner. Their aim is to be the ULTIMATE cat owner. The perfectionist will have done extensive research before acquiring a cat, using a detailed spreadsheet that cross-references the qualities required with those as advertised on various breeders' and rehoming charities' websites. This prospective owner will then approach the whole relationship with meticulous precision to make absolutely sure to be perfect in every respect. She will research the best diets, explore the indoor-versus-outdoor debate with vigour, contemplate the optimum litter-tray size, shape and substrate, and interview veterinary surgeons for suitable medical care. The perfectionist will always have the latest must-have piece of cat kit that is assured to make the cat's life complete. The medical notes for this cat will be extensively peppered with notes such as, 'Owner called to say cat sneezed. Gave advice to wait and see and report in 24 hours.' If you find yourself in the company of the perfectionist, DO NOT be tempted to demonstrate any of your new-found knowledge. She soaks up information and demands details just in case something you know could enhance her cat-owning capabilities. If this happens, you may end up floundering and making stuff up. She will suck you dry. Definitely don't ever suggest that her cat looks a little peaky or comment on the strong smell of urine in the dining room.

THE FEEDER

The feeder believes in the philosophy, 'I love, therefore I feed.' She loves her cat (or cats) so much that it is imperative she lets them know all the time. But this assurance often seems to fall on deaf ears, so she shows her love with food instead. The cat gets at least four set meals a day, plus a bowl of biscuits for snacking, plus treats (ham, cheese, kitty biccies, and prawns). Don't forget, of course, cooked white fish on Friday and roast chicken on Sunday, and the little bit of milk from her cereal every morning. The feeder believes that every time her cat makes a sound, it is saying, 'Feed me.' Any thought of denying that request would be criminal. After a few years of this, the cat spends most of the time indoors, seemingly because he loves her so much. In reality, he can no longer fit through the cat flap. Still she feeds and feeds, and when he struggles to get off the sofa, she finds a handy way to feed him 'in bed'. She has changed her vet several times as a few rude ones dared to tell her that her cat was dangerously obese. The feeder is the one who laughs in a loving way and says 'Aaaaaahhh' when she sees pictures of paunchy cats on the internet slouched on the sofa with a beer bottle and pizza propped up next to them. There are several words and phrases to avoid with the feeder: 'fat, overweight, morbidly obese, diabetic, prone to heart disease, and loved to death'. You will never change the feeder, but if you get the opportunity, you might want to at least try to reduce the poor animal's calorific intake.

THE MUST-HAVE OWNER

This is the person who is a designer-label slave. He has everything branded and is the personification of whatever he has decided is the fashion zeitgeist. A moggy is no match for this individual; he will have a

Savannah, a Bengal (F2 of course), a Sphynx (especially if he is follically challenged) or some other brand-new variation, particularly if it is rare and expensive. The must-have owner will import a Teacup (miniature) Persian from the States at great expense, only to find it's exactly like a normal Persian but has clearly been photographed from very far away. He will buy diamond-encrusted collars for his cat and obviously keep it (and the collar) indoors due to their high value. The cat will enjoy all the fancy mod-cons of urban cat indoor living (courtesy once again of the USA) but absolutely no opportunity to live a normal life. The must-have owner won't care what you know about cats because that sort of information just isn't useful or necessary, as his cat has been specially bred to live the way it does. It doesn't have a natural instinct in its body.

THE BUSY MUM

The busy mum will have several children and possibly several cats, but she's not absolutely sure whether she still has three or if Pickle has permanently decamped to the couple over the road. She acquired her cat as a kitten when her daughter came home one day demanding a cat and didn't stop until she got one. Since then, of course, mum has been in charge, but she's busy and didn't notice the promiscuous behaviour of her six-month-old cat who subsequently had three kittens, two of which she kept and called Branston and Pickle. The cats don't go to the vet (apart from when the mother was spayed, or 'spayed-ed' as the busy mum prefers to call it) as they don't get sick. They are either outside or inside, depending on whether they are noticed crying at the window outdoors or on the doormat indoors. The cats are invariably blissfully happy if they can get away from the youngest child's tormenting hands, but are often found dangling upside down as the enthusiastic child has picked them up back to front. Your expertise will not necessarily impress the busy mum, but this might be a good chance to see what cats get up to when they are given a measure of liberty and freedom of choice.

THE MAD CAT WOMAN

This type is part of a broad spectrum that starts with breeders and cat charity volunteers and ends in RSPCA interventions and court cases. You will never see the extreme end of the spectrum as it all happens behind closed doors; leave that to the real experts. However, you will undoubtedly have met 'types' from the other end in vast numbers. The mad cat lady charity volunteer, for example, is over 50, post-menopausal and largely suspicious of anyone who wants to come and adopt a cat, and positively aggressive to those who want to give them up. The mad cat woman will have at least six cats but possibly considerably more. These cats may or may not have their full quota of eyes, ears, limbs, etc. as they tend to be the ones that nobody else wants. Their owners have a uniform very much like that of the breeder (*see* 'Good Breeding') and all jewellery, handbags, pens, purses, key rings and (God forbid) tattoos will have a cat theme. Her house will be a homage to cat with every conceivable object either in the shape of a cat or adorned with a picture of one.

NORMAN AND NORMA

Norman and Norma are the statistical mean of the cat-owning population. They have had cats all their lives on and off and can always come up with an amusing anecdote of when the cat urinated on the vicar's lap or ate the Christmas turkey. They love their cats and care for them, but they have busy, independent lives outside their relationship with the cats and only ever occasionally consider buying something with a cat theme on it.

They put their cats out at night, give them milk and Maltesers, and do all the things that current wisdom suggests will kill them. Their cats usually live to 20. They might be briefly enthralled by your expertise, but are more likely to be impressed if you can recognise all 70 cultivated species of fuchsia.

FELINE FILLERS

The French philosopher Montaigne once mused: 'When I am playing with my cat, how do I know she is not playing with me?'

'Cats are rather delicate creatures and they are subject to a lot of ailments, but I never heard of one who suffered from insomnia.'

Joseph Wood Krutch, American writer and naturalist

THE CAT'S GOT *WHAT?*

HOW NOT TO LOOK LIKE AN IDIOT AT THE VET'S

First and foremost, you need to get a feeling for the whole medical thing. Cats get sick and, despite their nine lives, they get broken from time to time and need fixing. This is where the veterinary surgeon steps in.

Vets come in four guises:

1. **Large animal vet** Usually male, undoubtedly in a uniform of check skirt (sleeves rolled up), knitted tie and corduroy trousers, all of which are in the muted shades of the country (khaki, brown, beige, etc.).

2. **Horse vet** Dashing male or female, mixing with the rich and powerful of equine society and brave enough to diagnose and treat an animal worth more than most people would earn in a lifetime. (*See The Bluffer's Guide to Horseracing*).

3. **Small animal vet** A good mix of young and old,

but weighted towards young women of caring disposition, probably dressed in the corporate colours and uniform of the practice and largely passionate about dogs and cats (often placing themselves secretly in one camp or another).

4. **Exotic vet** Rarely exotic upon closer inspection. This is the vet who has, for whatever reason, decided to devote his or her life to tortoises, snakes, lizards, parrots, rats and virtually any other animal kept for fun or profit that isn't a dog or cat and doesn't live on a farm or in an equestrian centre.

Of the four vets above, you will rarely need to consider 1, 2 and 4, as the 'small animal vet' is the obvious choice to mend cats. Although vets are committed and generally well-liked servants of the community, many cat lovers find visits to their surgeries extremely stressful. Owners often complain of parting with a vast sum of money for a diagnosis they can't pronounce or a treatment protocol they don't understand. You cannot bluff a veterinary surgeon (why would you try?) but what you can do, if you ever find yourself in this situation, is hold your own and look like the intelligent layperson you are with just enough good knowledge to get by.

The vet is a Very Important Person in the life of the cat owner. Ironically, the most praise that he or she will receive from clients is when a beloved cat's life is ended through euthanasia. The term euthanasia is invariably not used in front of the owners, often replaced by the gentler euphemism 'putting to sleep'. Now this may seem strange, but the manner in which a vet performs this P-T-S (putting to sleep), and the empathy and compassion they show during and after it, will dictate how their abilities are judged by their clients. No amount of fancy diagnostic machinery or post-nominal letters will compensate for a 'bad' euthanasia. You could go down the route of feeling pretty sorry for the average vet experiencing that sort of performance pressure on a daily basis, but this probably won't help you in your role as a serious bluffer. It will, however, stand you in good stead if you refer to such musings should you ever meet a 'small animal' vet in a social situation. Never try to bluff a vet, but if you stick to the subject of 'grief management' and bereavement counselling, you'll be on safe ground. All good vets know the importance of this, and will generally be gratified to learn that their concern does not go unnoticed.

At some stage, as you mix more and more in the 'circle of cat', you are likely to find yourself called on to comfort someone in their hour of cat-related need. If this person has a cat that is sick or injured, then emotions will run high and someone (like you for example) needs to be there to be the cool, rational head who saves the day when all around are losing theirs. Here's what to do in a difficult situation at the vet's when someone you know is expecting what might be bad news.

- Be calm, polite and, above all else, rational. Remember that although you might be bluffing about the extent of your expertise on the subject of cats, this is not the time to continue the pretence. Do what you know is right in the circumstances.

- Don't be afraid to ask questions of the vet:

  o What are the differential diagnoses (what do you think might be wrong)?

  o What are the tests you need to do to establish the actual diagnosis?

  o How distressing may these tests be for the patient?

  o Depending on the diagnosis, what is the treatment and prognosis?

- Never say: 'I read on the internet that…'; this will drive the vet mad and alienate him or her immediately. Vets acquire their knowledge through years of study and practical experience. But however much they make it clear that they know their stuff, don't be fobbed off by someone saying, 'Because I said so.'

- Make notes about all the relevant things you need to know as you go along. This has the effect of making you look slightly more competent. Nonetheless, do your homework first so that you understand some of the more common things that might be wrong. The vet might be the sort that uses lay terms but, if not, you need to be up to speed.

- If you and the cat's owner are still unsure of the prognosis, suggest making another appointment to see the vet – but without the cat (which doubtless will come as a relief to the cat). The dynamics will be very different, and it is often much easier to communicate effectively in this less emotionally charged situation.

- If the vet is finding it difficult to make a diagnosis, in other words, if there is any hint of doubt, don't be afraid to request a second opinion or referral to a specialist. It's standard procedure under these circumstances and no vet will be offended. It will also make you appear very assertive and in control.

- It will do the bluffer no harm to commit to memory the following list of the most common diseases, injuries and symptoms to guide you through the minefield of veterinary terminology. You will need to get used to speaking in acronyms – no veterinary conversation is complete without a mention of F-E-L-V, F-I-V, F-I-P, F-I-C, F-O-R-L or I-B-D. Practise those in front of the mirror but don't ever consider trying to make words of 'Felv', 'Fiv' or 'Fip', etc. Nobody does this.

A LAYPERSON'S GUIDE TO VETSPEAK

These are arguably the most common diseases, symptoms and injuries that a cat might encounter. Commit them to memory and you won't look back.

Acute renal failure (ARF) Can occur as a result of an infection, toxin or blockage within the urinary tract.

Allergic flea dermatitis Itchy, scaly skin or fur loss caused by an allergy to flea saliva when bitten.

Arthritis (osteoarthritis) Inflammation of the joints causing pain and often resulting in restricted mobility. Joints affected are usually the hip, elbow and spine.

Blocked anal glands The anal glands are situated at '20 minutes to 4' (believe it or not there is a clock face on the cat's bottom). They contain fluid that occasionally builds up and causes discomfort, 'scooting' on the floor, and excessive and obsessive grooming around the anus. Ah, the joys of cat ownership.

Cat bite abscess Caused by another cat's bacteria-ridden canine teeth puncturing the skin during fights.

Cat flu/herpes/calicivirus This can be vaccinated against but will cause a snotty nose, runny eyes and ulcers on the tongue. Welcome to the wonderful world of cats.

Chronic renal failure (CRF) A condition usually seen in older cats, resulting in decreased appetite, weight loss and dehydration.

Conjunctivitis Inflammation of the pink bit around the eye causing pain, squinting, rubbing, discharge and reddening.

Detached retina Can be caused by high blood pressure, or a heavy bang on the head, often rendering the cat blind.

Diabetes Same as humans: drink a lot, pee a lot, eat a lot and lose a lot of weight (often due to amputation of a limb).

Diaphragmatic hernia More often than not caused by impact with a car which results in vital organs being radically relocated.

Ear mites Parasites that live in the ear canal and cause irritation, head shaking, dark brown wax and furious scratching.

Feline idiopathic cystitis (FIC) Stress-related inflammation of the bladder wall, causing pain, blood in the urine and even a complete inability to urinate.

Feline infectious peritonitis (FIP) A fatal disease caused by a type of virus called coronavirus. Best avoided.

Feline immunodeficiency virus (FIV) Caused by a similar retrovirus to HIV although it is not transmissible to man.

Feline leukaemia virus (FeLV) A viral condition that affects the immune system. You need to know that there is a vaccination that can protect against it.

Feline odontoclastic resorptive lesion (FORL) A hole in the bottom of the tooth at the gum margin that exposes the nerve. Usually accompanied by much yowling.

Food hypersensitivity This can manifest itself as an itchy skin condition, over-grooming, vomiting or diarrhoea. Welcome again to the world of cats.

Fractured mandibular symphisis A broken lower jaw; common in road traffic accidents.

Hyperthyroidism A tumour on the thyroid glands that causes an increase in the cat's metabolism. Usually accompanied by severe weight loss.

Hypertrophic cardiomyopathy (HCM) Heart disease that causes thickening of the wall of the heart. Believe it or not, some cats have hearts.

Inflammatory bowel disease (IBD) Causes diarrhoea, weight loss, vomiting and general loss of condition.

Lymphoma Cancer of the lymph nodes. Cats get cancer too.

Obesity You can't have a list without including fat cats. A major cause of heart disease, diabetes and joint problems through overeating/feeding. Killing with kindness is a serious problem in the cat world.

Pancreatitis Inflammation of the pancreas; as unpleasant as it is in the human pancreas.

Pelvic fractures These are commonly seen resulting from traffic accidents and falls.

Periodontal disease The build-up of plaque and tartar on the teeth, resulting in erosion and inflammation of the gums and loosening of the teeth. A cat with no teeth is not a happy cat.

Ringworm This is a skin infection caused by a fungus that is contagious to both cats and humans. Take advice from a real expert.

Squamous cell carcinoma (SCC) A type of cancer causing crusting of the ear tips, eyelids and nose; seen most commonly in cats with white ears and noses.

Tail pull injury This is commonly seen in cats that have been involved in traffic accidents or a cat that has attempted to withdraw a tail trapped in a door.

Urolithiasis Production of crystals in the cat's urine that merge to form stones in the bladder.

ALTERNATIVE AND COMPLEMENTARY THERAPIES

Cat lovers may also embrace alternative or complementary therapies. Just so you know, it wouldn't be unheard of for a cat to have physiotherapy, chiropractic treatment, acupuncture, osteopathy, herbal remedies, homeopathic remedies, acupressure, aromatherapy, reiki, Tellington Touch (touching and moving cats in particular ways to increase tolerance of human contact) and various food supplements to enhance health. Even so-called animal psychics are consulted by desperate owners seeking a solution to a problem. Best avoided.

FELINE FILLERS
Superstitions from around the world

1. A three-coloured cat will keep the house safe from fire (always encourage the more conventional use of a smoke detector alarm).

2. On every black cat there is a single white hair which will bring wealth or love to the person who removes it without the cat scratching them (don't try this at home, unless you believe that wealth and love can be found at A&E).

AND FINALLY...

To complete your training, you need to remember a couple of important rules: firstly, all cat lovers are kind and well-meaning. Though they frequently make great companions, you should never give one the ultimatum, 'It's me or the cat!' You are replaceable; the cat isn't. Secondly, a cat has the capacity to be anything a person wants it to be and is therefore the perfect partner – another human cannot do this, not even in a cat-themed 'onesie' with whiskers and silly ears, so please don't try.

If you find yourself, as you come to the end of this experience, whimsically searching YouTube for the latest footage of a cat playing a piano or hovering round the leopard-print soft furnishings in John Lewis, do not be alarmed. Ailurophilia is catching but not nearly as sinister as it sounds.

GLOSSARY

Activity centre Also known as an aerobic centre or cat tree. A form of modular scratching post (*see* below) that consists of numerous platforms, beds and perches at various levels. Calling it an aerobic centre is a misnomer, as a cat will rarely do more than sleep on it.

Adoption The acquisition of second-hand, pre-owned or unwanted cats or kittens.

Bath Somewhere to drink from or in which to torment spiders. NEVER to be used for the more conventional purpose where the average cat is concerned.

Breeder Someone who breeds specific cats (usually pedigrees) for financial gain, prestige or as a hobby. Considered by laypersons to be experts, as determined by the length of time they have been doing it or the number of kittens they produce at any one time. Neither are particularly good indicators of whether or not they know 'diddly squat' about cats.

Castrate To neuter a male cat by removing the testes via two small incisions in the scrotum and tying the remaining blood and semen carrying vessels in a knot (don't try this at home). Also known as 'fixed', 'knackered', or 'de-nutted'.

Cat basket Also known as cat carrier or box. This is made of wire, plastic, wicker or, rather foolishly, cardboard, and used to transport the cat securely from one location to another. Usually from home to vet's, and therefore deeply disliked.

Cat flap A small opening cut out of the bottom of the back door, enabling the cat to come and go without the owner acting as unpaid doorman. Usually results in every other cat in the neighbourhood coming and going too.

Catnip A dry form of the herb *Nepeta cataria*, which when eaten, inhaled or rolled in causes a euphoric state in many cats. Non-addictive and non-harmful, but can cause excessive drooling.

Diarrhoea Common in cats who eat too many treats or scavenge from bins. Often deposited in inappropriate places such as the owner's duvet or the hall carpet. Also referred to as 'intestinal hurry'.

Drinking fountain A commercial product that pumps water from a reservoir through a 'tap' to give a cat a source of running water. This is preferred by some and ignored by others in favour of the glass of water on the owner's bedside table.

Feral A domestic cat that lives in the wild. You may also hear the common malapropism 'febrile' and the just plain wrong 'ferile' when people talk about this subject, so don't get confused.

Fleas Small brown parasites that live in a cat's fur and lay eggs in the owner's carpet. Almost invisible to the naked eye, but detected if small black 'commas' are found in a cat's bedding. (Bluffers will know that if you place these on a piece of white paper and add a drop of water, they will turn red. This is the ingested blood of their host.)

Flehmen The 'faraway' look, involving a gaping mouth and vacant expression, that cats indulge in when 'tasting' smells with their vomeronasal organ.

Hairball Also known as a furball, this is a furry, sausage-shaped 'gift' vomited up by a cat, consisting of a compressed cocktail of ingested hair, food and spit. Usually found under the dining room table shortly before a dinner party.

Harness A leather device that fits around the cat's stomach and neck facilitating the attachment of a lead for walking in the park. It rarely results in a happy experience for owners or cats. The latter don't 'do' leads.

Kibble Also known as biscuits, nuggets, pellets, nuts. The small, dry, brown balls that pass for cat food; available in flavours of meat (beef, lamb, etc.) and bearing little resemblance to a cat's natural diet.

Litter The name given to a variety of commercially manufactured substrates designed to encourage a cat to deposit urine and faeces in an indoor tray. It can be made from wood, paper, corn, silica or Fuller's earth – all from sustainable sources, naturally.

Litter tray Also known as litter box or pan, this is traditionally a rectangular receptacle that contains litter (*see* above). There are now advanced self-cleaning and motorised models, both of which will guarantee that the cat will perform on the carpet instead.

Microchip A small rice-grain-sized chip inserted under the skin on the back of a cat's neck that, when scanned, provides information regarding the cat and its owner. Its principal purpose is to identify lost cats, but some even provide information about body temperature, thus eliminating the need to insert a thermometer rectally. Most cats are profoundly grateful for this function.

Obese A word not recognised by cat owners, who prefer to use the terms 'well loved', 'thick-furred' or 'big-boned'.

Predation The food chain in action. Otherwise known as inter-species murder.

Rescue A blanket term referring to organisations or individuals that rehome second-hand cats and unwanted kittens. It is also what cat counsellors can do for owners at the end of their tether.

Scooting The act of rubbing the bottom on the carpet with the back legs in the air while moving forward via a pulling action with the forelegs. Usually the consequence of an irritable anus due to worms or blocked anal glands.

Scratching post An object consisting of a post covered in sisal twine and a base covered in carpet provided for cats to scratch; generally ignored in favour of the sofa arm.

Scruff The loose skin at the back of a cat's neck that is grabbed by some misguided individuals to restrain an unwilling cat. The cat may be stilled for the moment, but it will harbour a grudge and undoubtedly act up if it ever meets the perpetrator again.

Spay To neuter (de-sex) a female cat by removing the ovaries and uterus; not always appreciated, but is said to extend a cat's life and obviate the ghastly process of going into 'heat'.

Spot-on The application of flea or worming treatment that requires the hair to be parted at the back of the cat's neck and a liquid deposited on the skin. Should really be called 'Splat-on' as in practice most of it ends up being applied randomly.

Tabby A common coat colour involving stripes, blotches or spots, and in various shades of brown, grey or ginger. In other words, a bit of a melange.

Tortoiseshell Also known as 'tortie', the tortoiseshell coat pattern is splashes of white, ginger and black or a dark mix of ginger and black flecks. Tortoiseshells are often referred to as 'naughty torties'.

Vaccination Something a cat needs yearly or (there is some debate over this) every three years. It protects the cat against some of the major infectious diseases but is rarely appreciated.

Valerian The root of the valerian plant, which has a catnip-like effect on some cats when added to toys, with the bonus of a jolly good snooze afterwards.

Vomiting Something cats do with great regularity after eating too much food, grass or their own fur. It is also a common symptom of many common cat illnesses. It is no coincidence that many cat owners opt for vomit-coloured carpets.

Worms Parasites that can be either round (long, thin and white) or tape (white and segmented), both infesting the cat's digestive tract and requiring regular worming treatment.

Zoonosis Any disease that can pass between human and animal. If in doubt, don't snog the cat.

A BIT MORE BLUFFING...

Available from all good bookshops

bluffers.com